How To Worship

Entering Into and Enjoying the Presence of God

Rev. Michael Dorsey

Volume 9 of the How To Live series

Unless otherwise indicated, all Scripture quotations are from The Holy Bible, English Standard Version® (ESV®), copyright © 2001 by Crossway, a publishing ministry of Good News Publishers. Used by permission. All rights reserved.

Scripture quotations marked NKJ are taken from the New King James Version® of the Bible. Copyright © 1979, 1980, 1982, 1983, 1984 by Thomas Nelson, Inc. Publishers. Used by permission. All rights reserved.

Scripture quotations marked KJV are taken from the King James Version of the Bible.

This book is part of the How To Live series:

volume 1   How To Study Your Bible
volume 2   How To Pray
volume 3   How To Be Blessed
volume 4   How To Please God
volume 5   How To Flow
volume 6   How To Get Healed
volume 7   How To Be Right
volume 8   How To Love
volume 9   How To Worship

How To Worship
Entering Into and Enjoying the Presence of God
ISBN 978-0-9916205-0-0

Copyright © 2014 by Robert Michael Dorsey

Published by Malakim Press
PO Box 456
Aberdeen, MD 21001

Cover art and design by Rose Watters

All rights reserved under International Copyright Law. Contents and/or cover may not be reproduced in whole or in part in any form without the express written consent of the Publisher except in use of a review.

*This book is dedicated to
my beautiful wife*

Mary Katherine Dorsey

*a faithful witness of the Lord
who believed in me long
before I ever believed in myself*

Acknowledgements

I would like to thank...

My Lord and Savior Jesus Christ - Thank You!
This book is from You, but it is also for You

Master Sergeant James Morris for our
many conversations and a kick in
the rear when I needed it

Susan Schuder for first teaching me
what worship is really all about

Pastor Jason Evans for your example of
excellence, your faithful support,
and your selfless friendship

All of my friends and Riverside Church family
for your sincere love and encouragement.

Thank you all so very much.

Table of Contents

Foreword 1

Introduction 5

Chapter One ...... In Spirit and In Truth 11
      The Nature of Worship

Chapter Two ...... What Are We Really Talking About?........... 21
      Defining Thanksgiving, Praise & Worship

Chapter Three ... You Are the Church 33
      The Place of Worship

Chapter Four ..... The Outer Court 43
      Practicing Worship

Chapter Five ...... The Inner Court 59
      Perfect Praise

Chapter Six .... The Most Holy Place 77
      Psalms, Hymns & Spiritual Songs

Chapter Seven ... Why Should We Do This? 93
      Motivation for Worship

Chapter Eight .... Getting Started 107
      Examples of Worship

Conclusion 119

Scripture Index 123

Foreword

Nothing is more frustrating than coming into a worship service at church and finding people standing around gawking at each other or staring blankly up at the ceiling. Don't even get me started on the "worshipers" that sit like spectators at a sporting event as though they were waiting for some great play to occur.

As a Lead Pastor, I sometimes feel for worship leaders and worship teams as they attempt to do the best they can to get us to move into a place of true and authentic worship. I have even found myself from time to time trying to encourage and motivate God's people to really worship. In my twenty plus years of serving the Lord in ministry as a Youth Pastor and Lead Pastor, I know and understand the value of how important it is to experience God in a worship service.

On more than one occasion I have stood in front of a congregation of worshipers, sensing that God was about to show up in a powerful and meaningful way, only to be missed because of a lack of true worship. I am a preacher and I love to preach, but in my experience I have seen more lives impacted and changed during the worship part of our services.

Worship is so vital to our church, and so near and dear to my heart, that I never want it to become just a "song service" when it should be "worship service." One time

How To Worship

while serving as Lead Pastor, our worship team at the time got off track and started to miss the importance of why and how we worship. It got so bad that during one of our Sunday morning church services the Holy Spirit spoke to me clearly and said that we had grieved Him that day. Shortly after that I had a meeting and dismissed the entire twenty plus member worship team including all of our musicians.

For the next eight to ten weeks, Sunday morning worship was limited to playing compact discs and DVDs during the worship time. I would then stand before a packed church and talk to them about what real worship is all about. Here it is now eight years later and people are still thanking me for following the leading of God and getting us back to a place of real worship.

The journey that this book is about to take you on will not only encourage and motivate you, but it will teach you HOW to worship our great and wonderful God. Michael Dorsey writes in a way that whether you are eight years old or eighty eight years young, you will understand the meaning of worship. Not only that, but you will also come to understand the connection to God that only worship can bring.

One of the things that I learned early in ministry was not to just give people theory and opinion, but rather to explain to them what God has to say about the subject or topic of which you are speaking. Reverend Dorsey has done just that with this book. He has taken God's Word on worship and given it handles so that we can put it to use. I have heard it said that information without application

Forward

is an abomination. Well, friend, get ready to become a worshiper that worships in spirit and in truth.

Your life is about to be forever changed and you are about to take your worship experience to another level. There will be no more coming into a worship service on Sunday morning as a "misplaced sporting spectator" or a "gawking saint." After you read this book you'll have no more excuses for why you don't "feel" God during the worship service. Oh, and the ceiling you've been blankly staring at on Sunday morning will give way to visions of heaven and to the glory of God. Who knows? You might come to church like Isaiah did and see the Lord high and lifted up with His train filling the temple. Enjoy!

Jason P. Evans
Ordained Minister, Church of God
Lead Pastor at Riverside Church, Aberdeen MD

Introduction

As the deer pants for the water brooks,
So pants my soul for You, O God.
My soul thirsts for God, for the living God.
When shall I come and appear before God?
– Psalm 42:1, 2 (NKJ)

Revival is sweeping across America and the entire world. You probably don't hear about it in the news media, but, by the power of the Gospel of Jesus Christ, tens of millions are being saved in Africa, South America, China, and many other nations. Here in the United States challenging economic conditions have helped many people realize they can't make it on their own, provoking them to seek help from God and leading them into church for the first time in their lives.

Unchurched people are more likely to be attracted to churches with lively worship services. However, they also discover that stepping into a Spirit-filled congregation can be quite a culture shock. They find that Christians have their own sub-culture and language, and it can be difficult to follow their terminology at times. Because these new believers have no religious background, they have many questions. In order to avoid appearing ignorant or foolish, they often will not seek answers from other lay

How To Worship

people or leadership within the church. Instead they just go with the flow, hoping to catch up somehow.

There are also many who do have some church background, but they are dissatisfied with the current state of their spiritual life. These are Christians who were raised in denominational churches, but in their heart they know there has to be more to the things of God than the dead, dry religious traditions they've been taught. They understand what Jesus meant when He told the Pharisees that their religious traditions made the Word of God to have no effect (Mark 7:13).

Many of these denominational Christians, tired of empty religious rituals, have also gravitated to Spirit-filled congregations. Seeking an encounter with the living God of the Bible, they have a strong desire to break free from the chains of man-made rules and routines, yet they also have many questions. Understanding the dangers of slipping into false doctrines and erroneous teachings, they don't want to trade one form of bondage for another.

Finally, there are Christians who have been involved with a Spirit-filled congregation from the beginning, enjoying the rich atmosphere of lively praise and worship along with anointed preaching and teaching. They're generally happy with where they are spiritually, but they know there are layers and depths of God they have yet to tap into, and they want to learn more.

Praise and worship is one of the most important aspects of your spiritual life, and there are already many wonderful books and teachings on the subject. However,

Introduction

most of these books focus on encouraging you to worship and motivating you to worship. They talk about why you need to worship, what worship will do for your life, how it's the will of God for you to worship, and how you need to start doing it.

What they don't tell you is how to worship. Believers everywhere are willing to worship God. They want to worship God. They just don't know how. They understand that it's important, but they don't know what to do. No one has ever taken the time to teach them, or been able to break it down in a way they can understand.

I experienced this myself as a young Christian. Saved in a Southern Baptist church when I was 10 years old, I became hungry for more of God and received the baptism of the Holy Spirit at the age of 16. I received very little help transitioning to a Spirit-filled congregation so I had to figure a lot of things out on my own.

By studying the Word of God and through the help of the Holy Spirit (John 14:26), all of my questions were eventually answered, yet it took a good long while. I really wish I would have had had a trustworthy resource to help me understand worship, or had been able to find someone who could show me what to do. Either source of help sure would have saved me a lot of time and frustration. That's the very reason *How To Worship* was written.

This book is directed toward both new believers and Christians who are seeking answers like I was, but more experienced Christians will benefit from reading it as well.

How To Worship

The Word of God is alive and inexhaustible on any subject, so you'll always walk away with some new nuggets of truth, even if you think you already understand a topic well. As you read this book, try to do so with an open and teachable heart. God's Word may possibly challenge some of your erroneous assumptions about worship, so as you read, you need to make an effort to stay open to the teaching ministry of the Holy Spirit.

May God richly bless you by granting you new insights and impartations of divine truth as you read, and may all of your questions about *How To Worship* be answered.

    Michael Dorsey

    March 2014

Let this be recorded for a generation to come, so

that a people yet to be created may praise the Lord:

that he looked down from his holy height;

from heaven the Lord looked at the earth,

to hear the groans of the prisoners,

to set free those who were doomed to die,

that they may declare in Zion the name of the Lord,

and in Jerusalem his praise,

when peoples gather together,

and kingdoms, to worship the Lord.

- Psalm 102:18-22

Chapter 1

In Spirit and In Truth
The Nature of Worship

"But the hour is coming, and is now here, when the true worshipers will worship the Father in spirit and truth, for the Father is seeking such people to worship him. God is spirit, and those who worship him must worship in spirit and truth."
 - John 4:23, 24

Jesus captured the essence of New Testament worship in John 4:24. As we begin this study on how to worship, what better place could we start than the words of our Lord Jesus Christ Himself?

He made this statement during a conversation with a Samaritan woman beside a well in the town of Sychar, where He was waiting for His disciples to rejoin Him. The Samaritans and the Judeans hated each other for many of the same reasons we find hatred in our world today: racial animosity and disputes over religion.

The racial animosity between their two peoples was based on a long list of historical grievances. The Judeans considered Samaritans unclean and looked down upon

How To Worship

them as inferior, and the Samaritans hated the Judeans for treating them so badly. The religious differences that separated them were even greater than their racial problems. The Samaritans made Mount Gerizim their center of worship. This caused the Judeans who worshiped in Jerusalem to hold the Samaritans in contempt. This was the context of Jesus' statement in John 4:23, 24.

The Samaritan woman was taken aback by a Judean like Jesus speaking to her, yet she soon became comfortable with Him and they struck up a conversation. It didn't take long for the subject to come back to religion and the controversy over how God should be worshiped. That's when Jesus began to speak about worshiping God in spirit and in truth. The Samaritan woman was wrapped up in religious technicalities, but Jesus was focused on the kind of worship God really wanted.

What does this have to do with us today? Whenever the subject of worship comes up, it seems as if people always want to get sidetracked with religious technicalities, just as the Samaritan woman did. They want to argue about such things as what style of music should be used, which instruments are acceptable and which ones aren't, or any number of other issues that have absolutely nothing to do with worshiping God in spirit and in truth.

Worshiping in spirit and in truth is what's important right now. Notice what Jesus said:

"But the hour is coming, AND IS NOW HERE, when the true worshipers will worship the Father in spirit and truth..." - John 4:23

In Spirit and In Truth

The time to start worshiping God is right now, today, but according to Jesus it must be done in spirit and in truth.

Worship in Spirit

So what does it mean to worship God in spirit? According to Jesus, the reason this is necessary is because God is a spirit. The only way we can commune with God is through our spirit, because He is a spirit.

Worship is a spiritual activity. It's not an endeavor of the mind or of the body. You can't reason your way in or physically exert yourself into worship. As we'll see later, the mind and the body are involved in worship, but worship is still a matter of the spirit.

Notice Jesus also said: "... *the TRUE worshipers will worship the Father in spirit and truth...*" If there are true worshipers that means there must also be false ones. The prophet Isaiah prophesied about false worshipers:

And the Lord said: "Because this people draw near with their mouth and honor me with their lips, while their hearts are far from me, and their fear of me is a commandment taught by men.
- Isaiah 29:13

These are people who seem to be going through the motions of worship outwardly, but in their hearts (their spirit) the truth is they aren't worshiping at all. Perhaps they're trying to impress someone or they're trying to fool the people around them, but they can't fool God. God sees everything. He knows the thoughts and intents of the heart, and He sees when our motives are wrong. The consequences of false worship are very serious:

> **For although they knew God, they did not honor him as God or give thanks to him, but they became futile in their thinking, and their foolish hearts were darkened. - Romans 1:21**

God demands authenticity from us. When we come into His presence to worship Him in spirit, we have to be real with Him. If we can't be honest when we stand before Him, we dishonor Him, and if we dishonor Him then our hearts will be darkened. That means we risk losing all of the spiritual insights and revelation that we have gained along the way so far.

Worshiping God in spirit means to worship Him with reverence, with the intention and purpose of honoring Him. When we come into His presence, we must always remember Who it is that we are actually approaching. He is holy. He's the God of the universe, the Judge of Heaven and Earth.

> **Therefore let us be grateful for receiving a kingdom that cannot be shaken, and thus let us offer to God acceptable worship, with reverence and awe, for our God is a consuming fire.**
> **- Hebrews 12:28, 29**

In order to worship God in the right spirit, we must take time before worship to prepare our hearts. Our worship must show great reverence toward God. He is our Creator and He holds our eternal destiny in His hands. We must strive to please Him.

> **For who in the skies can be compared to the Lord? Who among the heavenly beings is like the Lord, a God greatly to be feared in the council of the holy ones, and awesome above all who are around him? - Psalm 89:6-7**

Two great keys to spiritual growth are learning how to be brutally honest with yourself, and how to be brutally honest with God. God knows the thoughts and intentions of your heart anyway, so there's no need for pretense with Him, is there? Let us become "true worshipers" of Almighty God as we worship Him in spirit, so that He will always find our worship acceptable.

Worship in Truth

If worshiping God in spirit has to do with honesty and authenticity in our spirit-to-Spirit connection with Him, what does it mean to worship God in truth? We can gain some insight into the answer to this question from Jesus' prayer in John chapter 17, during the last supper, when He was praying for His disciples:

> **"Sanctify them in the truth; your word is truth."**
> **- John 17:17**

Jesus said that the Word of God is truth. When He says to worship God in truth, we could just as easily read it like this: *worship God in His Word.* In other words, worship God according to the Word of God. This may seem like an obvious and elementary point, but it's amazing how many people miss it.

There are many who think it really doesn't matter what you believe or do in church, just as long as you're sincere and follow your conscience. Yet, if it doesn't matter what you believe, then it really doesn't matter if you even believe at all. This absurd thinking exalts our conscience above the word of God. It makes our conscience our only guide and ignores what God says in the Bible.

We can't tell God that we're going to worship Him the way we choose, and that we really don't care what He has to say. If we did, every man would become his own authority, eliminating any need for the authority of God and His Word.

God has always told mankind how He is to be worshiped, but many people want to do what they think is best and what seems right to them. We are warned about this attitude in the book of Proverbs.

There is a way that seems right to a man, but its end is the way to death. Proverbs 14:12

We can lose our soul for eternity by doing what seems right in our own eyes, yet many insist on doing it anyway. This idea of doing what seems right in our own eyes has greatly affected the way people attempt to worship God.

When God's Word is no longer our guide, it always

In Spirit and In Truth

gets replaced with creeds, catechisms, disciplines, manuals, confessions, and other doctrines of men, who will justify their actions by simply rationalizing that God will accept them. This leads to people worshiping God in ignorance, just as Paul said of the Athenians, *"... whom therefore you ignorantly worship..."* (Acts 17:23 KJV).

When it comes to spiritual matters, the average person takes many things for granted. He finds certain religious groups practicing a certain way and he assumes that what the majority is doing must be right and acceptable to God. Yet the Bible says the majority of people are going to be eternally lost (Matthew 7:13-14), so we certainly don't want to depend on the majority to help us determine which way is right for us to follow!

One of the main reasons for the divisions observed within Christianity today is that man doesn't accept God's Word as final authority. Instead, stubborn humanistic man is determined to do it his own way. How important is it that we make sure our worship is in line with the Word of God? The Psalmist said:

I will worship toward Your holy temple, and praise Your name for Your lovingkindness and Your truth; For You have magnified Your word above all Your name. – Psalm 138:2 (NKJ)

A major reason we worship God is because of His truth. He has placed His Word at the highest level of importance, even above His name. If we're going to worship in truth, then we must not worship according to the religious conjecture of men. We must worship Him

How To Worship

the way His Word says to do so.

Many Christians who think they are worshiping God never stop to ask, "Is my worship scriptural? Is this what God wants?" Instead they act as though any kind of worship they give will be acceptable to God. However, God's Word has always made it plain that the only worship that is acceptable to Him is that which is in accordance with His written will.

Summary

In every age, God has specified how He is to be worshiped. We must worship God in spirit, with our hearts open and honest before Him, and we must worship Him in truth, operating in obedience to His holy written Word. We can't afford to be like the Samaritan woman, with a heart full of spiritual pride, lost in the religious legalism of man's ideas.

Jesus said in the Gospel of John that the hour is now here when the true worshipers will worship the Father in spirit and truth (John 4:24). I believe you want to be one of those true worshipers, or else you wouldn't be reading this book. Here is some really encouraging news from Jesus: He said that the Father is seeking such people to worship Him. That means God is looking for you!

Finally, notice that in John 4:24 Jesus said worshiping in spirit and in truth is the way we must do it. It's not optional. It's a command that we must obey if we want to please our Lord and Savior.

In Spirit and In Truth

What's really in your heart is a matter between you and God alone, and only you can make sure that your heart's motive is right. While you're taking care of that, in the coming chapters you'll be learning about worshiping God in truth. In other words, you'll begin to find out exactly what the Word of God has to say on the subject of How to Worship.

Chapter 1 Discussion Questions

1. Many church traditions were started by sincere people who sought to honor God. How do traditions lose their effectiveness? Is it possible to worship God through "traditional" worship?

2. Consider the influence of race, religion, and gender upon worship. How can cultural differences enhance or hinder the worship experience?

3. Quote: *"Two great keys to spiritual growth are learning how to be brutally honest with yourself, and how to be brutally honest with God."* Why do we sometimes struggle to be honest or transparent with the Lord and ourselves?

4. John 4:24 reveals God is SEEKING true worshipers. Why do you think true worship is paramount to God?

5. When a man cheats on a diet or on a test, who does that hurt the most? If a woman appears to be worshiping outwardly, but in her heart she is not, who does that hurt?

6. Another term for reverence is "godly fear." What does a reverently fearful attitude toward God look like? What does it sound like?

Chapter 2

What Are We Really Talking About?
Defining Thanksgiving, Praise and Worship

Enter his gates with thanksgiving,
And his courts with praise!
Give thanks to him; bless his name!
- Psalm 100:4

You have purposed in your heart to approach God and to begin worshiping Him, and you've committed to do it the way Jesus said you must: in spirit and in truth. Now what is the next step in learning How to Worship?

What can a man give to the Lord? Think about that for a moment. God has given us everything. He sent His Son to save us. He's given us His Word, including over 7000 promises of healing, provision, wisdom, joy, peace and the anointing of His Holy Spirit. He's given to us "... *all things that pertain to life and to godliness...*" (II Peter 1:3). What can we possibly give him in return?

There's absolutely nothing that He needs. Seated on His throne at the center of the Holy City in Heaven, He has want of nothing. The only thing He desires is for us to spend eternity with Him there, but even then that's not something He needs. God doesn't need you, but He does want you.

So again I ask: what can you give to God? He doesn't need your money. He doesn't need your efforts. If you won't serve Him then He'll find someone else that can do the job He wanted you to do. What does He want that only you can bring to Him? The answer is your praise. You can bring the same thing that the psalmist brought when he came to worship.

I will thank you in the great congregation; in the mighty throng I will praise you. - Psalm 35:18

The Bible talks about thanksgiving, praise, and worship. All worship of God will consist of these three steps in some form. These three are all similar to each other, yet each one is also distinct in its particulars. You might think of them as different levels or degrees of worship. In order to better understand thanksgiving, praise and worship, the first thing that must be done is to define them.

Thanksgiving

Thanksgiving means thanking God for the things He has done for you. That may seem like a very elementary concept, but thanksgiving goes deeper than you think.

In that day you will say: "Give thanks to the LORD, call on his name; make known among the nations what he has done, and proclaim

What Are We Really Talking About?

that his name is exalted. - Isaiah 12:4

Prayer in its most basic definition is a person communicating with God. There are many different kinds of prayer taught in the Bible, but thanksgiving, praise and worship are the highest forms of prayer you can make. In the prayer of thanksgiving you come before God, not to seek something new for yourself, but instead to bring one of the very few things you're truly capable of giving Him: your thanks.

Thanksgiving simply means thanking God for all of the things He has done for you. The focus of thanksgiving isn't on how great the need was, but on the greatness of the thing that was done. For example, you might thank God for your salvation, healing, answered prayer, deliverance from danger, or any number of things He's done in your life. If you've never done this before, I highly encourage you to try it.

I will give to the Lord the thanks due to his righteousness, and I will sing praise to the name of the Lord, the Most High. - Psalm 7:17

I remember the first time I intentionally prayed the prayer of thanksgiving. I said to myself, "I'm going to set aside this time to come before the Lord in prayer, and I'm not going to ask him for anything, not one single thing. For this prayer session, instead of focusing on me and my needs, I'm only going to thank Him for all the things He's done for me.

I started by getting my body still and my mind

How To Worship

quiet, blocking out the distractions of the day. Then I thought about some things I could thank God for. The first thing that came into my mind was my salvation, so I prayed, "God I thank you for saving me. I thank you for sending your Son to spill His precious blood, that the price for my sins might be paid so I can spend eternity with you."

Then I thought about something else I could thank Him for, so I thanked Him for that. Then I thought about the next thing I was thankful for, and I thanked Him for that. As I started to get into it, all the things I could be thankful for started coming into my mind more quickly. As I was speaking out one thing I found myself already thinking about the next thing I would say, so there weren't any pauses between my thanksgivings.

Then thoughts of things to thank Him for started coming even faster. As I was praying out one thing, I'd have two more in my mind to thank Him for after that. As I thanked him for the first of those two things, two more things would come into my head. I started talking faster so I could keep up with all the things that were coming to me to be thankful for.

Before I knew it, I found myself praying out the next thing while I was trying to keep five or six more things straight in my head to thank Him for, like people waiting in line to check out at a store. Then I started remembering even more things I could thank Him for, and they started coming to me even faster. I realized I wasn't going to be able to keep up with everything that was coming to me to be thankful for. It was too much.

What Are We Really Talking About?

As I completely lost control of that thanksgiving prayer, I was reduced to tears. I recognized the enormity of God's goodness toward me, and how He'd been so good to me that when I purposed in my heart to rehearse it back to Him I literally could not keep pace with all the things He's done to bless my life. It was a life changing experience for me.

If you try this you might not have an experience as emotional as mine was, and that's okay. The intent of giving thanksgiving to God isn't to have an emotional experience, but to make a spiritual connection with our Creator, Savior, Lord, Healer, Provider, Protector, and so on. Worshiping in truth means we judge our worship according to the Word of God, not based on personal experiences, but many times your emotions will also be involved.

Praise

Thanksgiving is thanking God for the things He has done for you, and the focus of thanksgiving is on the greatness of the thing that was done. Praise is similar to thanksgiving, but rather than thanking Him for the thing that was done you are praising the One who was the doer of the thing that was done.

> **Who is like You among the gods, O Lord? Who is like You, majestic in holiness, Awesome in praises, working wonders? - Exodus 15:11**

Praise is one level higher than thanksgiving in

terms of intensity. For instance, it's one thing when your boss gives you an extra assignment and when it's done he says, "Thanks for doing that." It's another thing when he tells you, "Hey, you did a really good job on that. You got it to me on time and it looked great. That was excellent work."

We can easily understand the difference when it comes to thanking and praising each other. The principle is exactly the same when it comes to thanking and praising God. You might thank God, "Lord I thank you for sending an answer to my prayer," and then praise Him by saying, "You are mighty. You've never let me down and You never will because you are so faithful."

Praise and thanksgiving often work together. There are many places in the Bible where they both appear in the same verse, yet they still serve two distinct purposes. *Thanksgiving recognizes the deed done, and praise glorifies the doer of the deed.*

> **Save us, O Lord our God, and gather us from among the nations, that we may give thanks to your holy name and glory in your praise.**
> **- Psalm 106:47**

Another way to understand praise is to think of it as an appraisal. When a house is going to be sold, the buyer has it appraised. The appraiser comes to the house, looks everything over, and determines what that house is truly worth. Finally, he delivers his report of the appraisal so that anyone who's interested can know the true worth of that house.

What Are We Really Talking About?

When you praise God you're doing the same thing. You're looking Him over, reviewing all the things that have happened with Him in your life, and then delivering your appraisal – your report of what He is truly worth to you. At the same time, your "appraisal" of praise will let all the people around you know what He's worth as well when they hear you praising Him.

But we your people, the sheep of your pasture, will give thanks to you forever; from generation to generation we will recount your praise. - Psalm 79:13

Worship

Worship takes thanksgiving and praise one level higher. It's a more intimate and personal experience than praise and thanksgiving, although once again they are all very similar and flow into one another.

Thanksgiving and praise deal with the things God has done, but worship deals with Who He IS. We worship God not for the goodies He brings us, but for the excellence of the quality of His intrinsic nature. Worship goes deeper than praise and thanksgiving.

All the nations you have made shall come and worship before you, O Lord, and shall glorify your name. For you are great and do wondrous things; you alone are God. - Psalm 86:9, 10

The word "worship" is a modern version of the Old

How To Worship

English word "worthship" which is made from two Old English words: *weorth,* which means "worth," and *scipe,* which means something like shape or "quality."

Similar to the "appraisal" of praise, worship has to do with how much God is worth. In material terms the worth of God is infinite and limitless because He created the material world. But the focus of worship is on the personal level: not just on how much God is worth, but how much is He worth to you?

The Old English suffix "–ship" is found in words like friendship and sportsmanship. Friendship describes the intrinsic nature of being a good friend. When talking about a person who demonstrates good sportsmanship, we're talking about the quality of being a good sport.

When these two words are put together, we get worship (worth-ship), which describes the intrinsic nature or quality of what God is worth. Another way you'll often hear this said is in the phrase "He is worthy."

> **Then I looked, and I heard the voice of many angels around the throne, the living creatures, and the elders; and the number of them was ten thousand times ten thousand, and thousands of thousands, saying with a loud voice:**
>
> **"WORTHY is the Lamb who was slain**
> **To receive power and riches and wisdom,**
> **And strength and honor and glory and blessing!" - Revelation 5:11, 12**

What Are We Really Talking About?

We worship God because He alone is worthy of worship. The reason idolatry is such a pitiful sin is because the people committing it are trying to claim that their idol is worth as much as God is worth. An idol could be a job, or a relationship, or a car, or almost anything.

We laugh at ancient peoples worshiping their little statues, but when we recognize that we can make idols out of almost anything in our lives, suddenly it's not so funny. What job is worth as much as the Almighty? What relationship should be accorded the same worth as Him? What material thing is worthy of your time and attention as much as He is worthy?

We need to clearly understand that there is nothing in our lives that has the same level of quality and intrinsic worth as the Lord does. God alone is worthy. He is the only one – the ONLY one – worthy of our worship.

Summary

Most people think of "worship" in general as an all-inclusive word that includes thanksgiving, praise and worship, and that's true. In fact, that's what I've done with the title of this book. However, it's also important to understand that while all three of these are similar phases of worship, each is distinct in its own way.

Thanksgiving focuses on the external things in your life, "What has God done for ME?" Praise is also about what He's done, but it's more intimate and not necessarily so much about us. Worship is the most intimate of the three, and it isn't about us at all.

How To Worship

Thanksgiving, praise and worship are three levels within the realm of worship in general, each one deeper than the one before it. Thanksgiving, praise and worship were separated for the purpose of studying them, but now that the differences between these three are understood, it's important that they are placed back together.

It's fine to look at them separately, but when isolating them for analysis it's important not to get overly clinical about it. Thanksgiving, praise and worship are different from one another, but they exist alongside each other, and oftentimes they will overlap. Many times in scripture two of them are mentioned together within the same verse.

In general, worship is a flow, and while it's acceptable to separate out these three elements to learn more about them, the truth is they flow together. When you worship God, there is a natural movement from thanksgiving, to praise, and then to worship.

Sometimes you'll go backwards from worship to praise, or from praise to thanksgiving. Other times you might skip praise and go straight from thanksgiving to worship. There's no right or wrong way to worship in that sense because worship isn't something that you do mechanically. Worship is a flow.

Now that the nature of worship (in spirit and in truth) and the general elements of worship (thanksgiving, praise and worship) are understood, the next thing to look at is this: Where do we worship?

What Are We Really Talking About?

Chapter 2 Discussion Questions

1. How is thanksgiving related to humility? How can the intentional daily praise of God and man foster an attitude of meekness within us?

2. Sometimes a person will say she's "very thankful" for something or "a little bit thankful" for something else. Does scriptural thanksgiving have degrees of intensity, or is it more of an attitude that either you are or are not thankful?

3. What is the difference between thanksgiving and praise? How does it help us to understand the distinction between the two?

4. What is the difference between praise and worship? Why is it helpful to know the difference between them?

5. How does worship inspire us to look more intently at God? How does it inspire you to examine yourself more closely?

6. Quote: *"Worship is a flow."* Does that mean it's always easy to do? How much discipline and effort does it take to really engage in worship?

Chapter 3

You Are the Church
The Place of Worship

I bow down toward your holy temple and give thanks to your name for your steadfast love and your faithfulness, for you have exalted your word above your name. - Psalm 138:2

God has always wanted to dwell with His people, ever since they were first separated from Him in the Garden of Eden. In Exodus chapter 25, God began to give Moses the plans to a holy meeting place. It was called the Tabernacle.

Tabernacle means "tent," "place of dwelling" or "sanctuary." As tents go, it was extremely fancy. If you wanted to build the Tabernacle today, as it is described in the book of Exodus, it would cost over 100 million dollars. God knew that the Israelites needed visual evidence of His presence, and no expense was spared when it was built.

The Tabernacle was the sacred place that God chose to meet His people, the Israelites, during the 40 years they wandered in the desert under Moses' leadership. It was the place where the leaders and people came together to worship and offer sacrifices.

Many years later, King David had it on his heart to build God a more permanent dwelling place. As amazing as the Tabernacle was, David wanted to give God a place that was even better. He spent the last years of his life gathering the necessary materials, and then his son, King Solomon, took over the project and completed the Temple in Jerusalem.

The Old Covenant Temple

Both the Tabernacle and the Temple of Jerusalem were divided into three sections: the Outer Court, the Inner Court which was sometimes called the Holy Place, and finally the "Holy of Holies," which was also referred to as the Most Holy Place. Stepping though the Temple gate, the first area one would encounter was the Outer Court.

This is the only place in the Temple where Gentiles were allowed. They couldn't go in any further. There were two pieces of furniture in the Outer Court: the Bronze Altar and the Laver. The Bronze Altar is where sacrifices were made, pointing ahead to the shed blood of Jesus Christ (Hebrews 9:12-14). The Laver is where the priests washed. It represented cleansing by the Word of God (Ephesians 5:26).

Next was the Inner Court, or the Holy Place, which was the middle section between the other two areas. Only Israelites could enter the Inner Court. Gentiles were prohibited from entering. This was a type of Christ's ministry of intercession, for it is only through Him that we can pass through the Veil that separated the Inner Court from the Holy of Holies (Matthew 27:50, 51).

The Inner Court area was furnished with the Table of Shewbread, the Lampstand, and the Altar of Incense. Twelve loaves were placed on the Table of Shewbread each week for God's enjoyment. This represents our fellowship with Christ (John 6:35). The Lampstand held oil, a symbol of the Holy Spirit. We praise God in the language we understand but also in other tongues by the Spirit (I Corinthians 14:15). The Altar of Incense represents the prayers of the saints (Revelation 5:8) and Christ's intercession for us (Ephesians 5:2).

After the Inner Court came the Holy of Holies, also known as the Most Holy Place. This was a room that only the High Priest was allowed to enter, and then only once per year on the Day of Atonement. This was the room where God dwelled (Exodus 25:8). The Holy of Holies included the Ark of the Covenant and the Mercy Seat.

The Ark of the Covenant contained a gold jar of manna, Aaron's staff that had budded, and the stone tablets of the Ten Commandments (Hebrews 9:3, 4). The Mercy Seat was the seventh piece of furniture in the Tabernacle, the number representing completion. This was the most important object in the sanctuary and the focus of all the attention, because it was at the Mercy Seat where the *Shekinah* glory presence of God appeared between the cherubim (Exodus 37:6-9).

God intentionally designed the Temple so that everything in it was a type and shadow of the Christ who was to come. It was one of the most amazing buildings in the ancient world. However, today He is worshiped in a structure that's even more impressive.

Understanding The New Covenant Temple

Today God is still worshiped in a temple, but it's not a physical building. When Paul was writing to the church at Corinth, he was surprised they didn't already realize this.

> **Do you not know that you are God's temple and that God's Spirit dwells in you? If anyone destroys God's temple, God will destroy him. For God's temple is holy, and you are that temple. - I Corinthians 3:16, 17**

The New Testament was originally written in Greek. The Greek for "you" is plural in verse 16 and 17 above. The word "temple" here is really all the people of God collectively. The Apostle Peter, after referring to Jesus Christ as the chief cornerstone of this temple, builds on this thought further:

> **You yourselves like living stones are being built up as a spiritual house, to be a holy priesthood, to offer spiritual sacrifices acceptable to God through Jesus Christ. - I Peter 2:5**

The church, the called out people of God, make up the New Testament temple. Each person in the church is one of the "living bricks" that together make up this spiritual building. The church isn't the building where you go, it's the brothers and sisters you know.

However, you don't have to be among your fellow believers to be "in the temple." The New Covenant temple is with you wherever you are, even if you're all by yourself. Not only is the church as a whole considered the living temple today, but your own body is a temple as well.

Or do you not know that your body is a temple of the Holy Spirit within you, whom you have from God? You are not your own, for you were bought with a price. So glorify God in your body.
- I Corinthians 6:19-20

What makes your physical body a temple? A temple is the place that houses the presence of God. Your body is a temple because the Holy Spirit lives inside it alongside your own spirit, just as He lives in the church as a whole.

This is what defines the New Testament temple. The "temple" of God is no longer a stone building as it was in the Old Testament. It's a spiritual building made up of living stones. Under the New Covenant, WE are the temple of God, and YOU are the temple of God.

Spirit, Soul and Body

When God created Adam from the dust of the earth (his body) and breathed the breath of life (his spirit) into him, then man became a living soul (Genesis 2:7). Created in God's image, man is also a three-part being consisting of spirit, soul and body.

How To Worship

Now may the God of peace himself sanctify you completely, and may your whole spirit and soul and body be kept blameless at the coming of our Lord Jesus Christ. - I Thessalonians 5:23

Your spirit is the real you, the part that will live somewhere for eternity. Your body is like a vehicle for your spirit. It's the part of you that allows you to interact with the physical world. Where your body and spirit come together is your soul, which consists of your mind, will and emotions. A phrase to help you easily remember this is: "I am a spirit, I possess a soul and I live in a body."

This three-part being corresponds to the three sections of the Old Testament Temple, and it also matches with the three levels of worship introduced in chapter two: thanksgiving, praise and worship. Let's take a closer look at these correlations.

The Outer Court

The Outer Court represents the body or the "flesh realm." This is where we enter with thanksgiving.

Blessed is the one you choose and bring near, to dwell in your courts! We shall be satisfied with the goodness of your house, the holiness of your temple! - Psalm 65:4

Step 1 of worship is to physically deliver yourself to the place of worship, whether that's going to a church to worship corporately with a congregation or going into a quiet room to worship alone. You must "bring your self" to that place.

Sometimes the flesh doesn't feel like giving thanks. It can be a sacrifice at first, but by making the sacrifice of praise (the Bronze Altar) you are cleansed from the corrupting influences of the world (the Laver), enabling you to proceed into the Inner Court.

The Inner Court

The Inner Court, also called the Holy Place, represents the soul or the "emotional realm." This is where we transition from thanksgiving into praise.

Enter into His gates with thanksgiving, and into His courts with praise. - Psalm 100:4

Israelites could enter the Holy Place, but Gentiles could not. A covenant relationship with the Lord is required to enter the Inner Court. It is the mid-point, where our inner man begins to be involved in the process.

You've moved past the flesh realm and you're now working on focusing and centering your thoughts on Him. This is where fellowship (the Table of Shewbread), communion with the Holy Spirit (the Lampstand), and prayer (the Altar of Incense) begin to happen.

The Most Holy Place

Finally you enter the Holy of Holies, where your spirit is able to transition from praise into worship. In the Temple of Jerusalem, the Inner Court was separated from the Holy of Holies by a giant curtain over thirty feet high, weaved to a thickness of more than three feet.

When Jesus died on the cross, this massive curtain was torn in half from top to bottom (Matthew 27:50-51), symbolizing that Christ's victory over sin meant there would no longer be any barrier between the presence of God and His people.

Not with the blood of goats and calves, but with His own blood He entered the Most Holy Place once for all, having obtained eternal redemption. - Hebrews 9:12

Your spirit-man corresponds to the Holy of Holies. This is the place where your spirit comes into communion with the Holy Spirit and where you can personally encounter the very presence and glory of God.

Summary

Exploring the fascinating intricacies of the Tabernacle and the Temple of Jerusalem, we find many parallels between the Temple's blueprint and God's architecture of man (body, soul and spirit). One could fill a library with the books that have been written expounding on this subject and the truths that can be found within it. The most basic points have been outlined here for the purposes of this study on How To Worship.

To review, the physical body is the Outer Court of the New Covenant temple, corresponding with the spiritual expression of thanksgiving.

The soul realm (the mind, will and emotions) is the Inner Court of your temple, and that is the part of you that matches up with the spiritual expression of praise.

The spirit-man is the Holy of Holies within this temple that is your body, corresponding with the expression of worship.

If you are a Christian, then the New Covenant temple is the place where worship happens. This is not a physical building, but a spiritual structure, composed of the church as a whole, but also represented in your three-part being that's been created in God's image.

In the next few chapters we're going to examine worship in a much greater degree of detail for each part of your temple, beginning with the Outer Court.

Chapter 3 Discussion Questions

1. What are some of the implications of your body being a temple of the Holy Spirit? What impact does that have on worship?

2. What parallels can we draw between the physical temple and the spiritual temple when we consider:

    - The value of the temple?
    - The layout of the temple?
    - The furniture of the temple?

3. How does understanding the symbolism and the layout of the Tabernacle relate to your thanksgiving, praise and worship experience?

4. Gentiles weren't allowed to enter the Inner Court. What is a Gentile? What is a covenant relationship, and how is it different from other relationships? How does a covenant relationship affect praise and worship?

5. If your spirit is the "real you," how does that impact your understanding of what it means to "worship God in spirit" (John 4:24)?

6. It's very common for people to discipline their bodies by going to the gym, or to discipline their minds by going back to school for additional education. Do you usually see people exercising the same kind of discipline on their spirits? What does spiritual discipline look like? How would it help us in the realm of praise and worship?

Chapter 4

The Outer Court

Practicing Worship

Let us go to his dwelling place;
Let us worship at his footstool!
- Psalm 132:7

  Walking up to the front door of the church on Sunday morning, the greeters give you a smiling welcome. Your own fake smile is pasted to your face as you tell them good morning. You normally prefer to arrive at church a little early, but now the service is just about to start. You're late because you got into an argument with your spouse over some stupid, foolish point that took up way too much time this morning. On the way to church the kids started bickering in the car and you had to raise your voice, further souring your mood. Now you have to hurry to get them checked into children's church, with no time to stop and visit with anyone you'd like to talk with. By the time you enter the sanctuary, the first song has already started. As you look for a place to sit, the usher greets you with a smile and a hearty handshake. You smile weakly in return, find a place to sit and start clapping your hands to the beat of the music. You are still frustrated that you were late but you are thankful to finally be in the worship service.

How To Worship

Welcome to the Outer Court of the New Covenant temple. The Outer Court represents the body or the "flesh realm." You aren't going anywhere on this planet without bringing your body along, so even though worship is primarily a spiritual experience, you're going to have to figure out what to do with your body.

Getting There

You must be brought to the place of worship before you can assume the posture of worship. Therefore the first step in the process of how to worship is to physically deliver yourself to the place of worship. That may sound like a very basic point but it can't be overlooked. You must pass through the Outer Court before you can get to the Inner Court and into the Most Holy Place.

The Outer Court is where you enter with thanksgiving. Sometimes the flesh doesn't feel like giving thanks at first, but you can push past that and start giving thanks anyway. The Bible talks about bringing the sacrifice of praise.

> **Therefore by Him let us continually offer the sacrifice of praise to God, that is, the fruit of our lips, giving thanks to His name. - Hebrews 13:15**

Why is it a sacrifice? Because honestly, sometimes you just don't feel like doing it, and when you feel that way it's usually easier to stand and watch than it is to start participating. Do it anyway. Start worshiping God with thanksgiving, whether you're "feeling it" or not.

The Outer Court

You can bring your body into a state of worshiping God no matter where you are. It can seem easier on a Sunday morning when you're in a church full of people all trying to move in the same direction with you. Lively music and the energy of the congregation are a great help in motivating you to get yourself going in worship.

You can also do the same thing when you are at home all by yourself. You can start up a favorite praise CD or mp3 playlist to help you along. In some ways it's more challenging because you don't have the crowd and the loud music motivating you, but it can also be easier in a sense because you don't have the distraction of those other people either.

There is nothing that will help you get into a state of worship faster than anointed music played with skillful excellence. Anointed music is a part of the Ministry of Helps (I Corinthians 12:28), and music can be a very big help to you as you enter the Outer Court of your temple.

However, you don't want to let music become a crutch, to the point that you can't worship if the praise band or the CD player is absent. Music will be examined in much greater depth in chapter 6, but for now just understand that the practical information on how to worship that you're learning in this book will work whether there's a praise band playing or not. Music can help you enter into worship but it's not a requirement, so make sure you don't let yourself become overly dependent on it.

The first step toward worshiping at the Holy of Holies is to enter the temple's Outer Court. Since you are the New Testament temple, and your body is the Outer Court, that means you must "bring yourself" to that place. Whether that's going to a church to worship corporately with a congregation or going into a quiet room to worship alone, you have to get yourself there.

Outward Displays of Worship

Now that you've brought yourself to the place of worship, you're ready to begin assuming the "postures of worship." Worship is an experience that involves every part of your temple: your body (Outer Court), your soul (Inner Court), and your spirit (Holy of Holies). While it's primarily a spiritual experience, you are still a three-part being created in God's image, and every part of you can be and should be involved in praise and worship.

Your body shouldn't just sit there like a pew potato while your inner man worships. It has its own unique role in the worship process. We can see this in the behavior of the Israelites when they worshiped:

> **Praise the Lord! Sing to the Lord a new song, and His praise in the assembly of saints. Let Israel rejoice in their Maker; Let the children of Zion be joyful in their King. Let them praise His name with the dance; Let them sing praises to Him with the timbrel and harp. For the Lord takes pleasure in His people; He will beautify the humble with salvation. - Psalm 149:1-4**

The Israelites were very demonstrative and outwardly expressive when they worshiped. There were different things they did with their bodies as they worshiped, and you can express yourself in worship using your body in the very same ways. Let's look at some of these postures of worship.

Standing

> **Praise the Lord!**
> **Praise the name of the Lord,**
> **give praise, O servants of the Lord,**
> **who stand in the house of the Lord,**
> **in the courts of the house of our God!**
>   **– Psalm 135:2**

Standing before the Lord is a posture of worship. As a general rule, when worshiping Him you should be standing. There are times when an individual won't be able to stand, or will be able to stand for only a short period of time. The point of listing these postures of worship isn't to condemn anyone, but rather to make you aware of what the Scriptures say we should be doing. If you're able to stand up during worship, you ought to be standing.

Standing demonstrates respect. Think about how everyone will rise when a high ranking individual, such as the President of the United States, enters a room. This is an outward recognition of the superior authority of that person. How much greater should our respect be for the King of Kings and the Lord of Lords?

Standing also conveys alertness. Have you ever seen someone fall asleep during worship? I have! In fact, there

How To Worship

have been some church services in which I've been so tired that I felt like dozing off. That's a lot harder to do when you're standing up though. Also, sometimes your mind will wander during worship. Standing will help keep your body alert, and when your body is alert it's easier to keep your mind alert as well.

Finally, standing shows expectation. Have you ever been to a concert where everyone was seated waiting for it to start, and then as the countdown began everyone started getting excited and standing up? Maybe you've been to a parade or a magic show where people behaved in a similar way. They wanted to make sure they didn't miss anything, so they stood up. Standing is a posture of worship that conveys respect, alertness and expectation.

Clapping

Clap your hands, all peoples!
Shout to God with loud songs of joy!
- Psalm 47:1

This is a posture of worship that almost everyone is comfortable with. Unlike singing or dancing, very few people will have a problem with clapping. Clapping is probably the easiest outward expression of worship there is, and that's where you have to be careful with it. It can actually be too easy. When you're clapping along with the music, it can be very easy to let yourself start drifting.

Clapping is so common to us that we do it without thinking about it, and so when we clap during worship it's easy to accidentally start worshiping without focusing

The Outer Court

on what we're really doing. Also, because clapping is such a common cultural expression here in the United States, we have to be careful when we're clapping in church that we don't slip into clapping toward God as though He were something equally common.

For example, clapping is something that happens at a concert or a sporting event. I might clap hard at the end of a concert performance that involves one of my children, or cheer loudly when my favorite team scores, but I need to be careful I'm not in that same mental frame when I'm clapping at church, because God doesn't belong in the same category as a performer or a sports star. He's not common at all.

Interestingly, of all the postures of worship listed in this chapter, clapping is the one that appears only in the Old Testament. There is no mention of clapping in the New Testament. This is another reason why clapping is probably the least of the various postures of worship. Instead, the New Testament gives us something else to do with our hands.

Lifting Holy Hands

I desire therefore that the men pray everywhere, lifting up holy hands, without wrath and doubting; - I Timothy 2:8 (NKJ)

Lifting your hands during worship demonstrates two major spiritual truths. The first is surrender. No matter where you are in the world, putting your hands in the air is universally recognized as the symbol for

How To Worship

surrendering. When you lift your hands before God in worship, you're saying to Him, "I surrender. I surrender to your Word. I surrender to your will. I surrender to your plan for my life."

The second thing that lifting your hands communicates is, "I receive." If I held out a twenty dollar bill to you and said, "Here, take this," then you would have to reach out to receive it. You'd reach across to me because I'd be right next to you. But what if I was halfway up the stairs and I leaned down to give it to you? You'd have to reach up vertically in order to get it from me. God is also above, and He has much better gifts for you than a twenty dollar bill.

Every good gift and every perfect gift is from above, coming down from the Father of lights with whom there is no variation or shadow due to change. - James 1:17

By lifting your hands, you're reaching up to receive by faith the things God has freely given you. Sometimes we don't feel like we deserve all of the gifts God has given us. We forget that what we deserve has absolutely nothing to do with it, but that it's only by the blood of Jesus Christ that we're able to receive eternal life and everything else He's provided for us. Don't be focused on whether you deserve it or not – because you don't – and just reach up to receive it anyway.

Some people feel self-conscious about lifting their hands in church, but you have to remember who is the One you want to impress. I call this the Audience Principle of

The Outer Court

worship. If we're not careful, we'll think of the praise team on the platform as the performers and ourselves as the audience, but that isn't accurate at all.

What's really happening is the praise team is leading the congregation and both are performing the worship, and God is the true audience. Remembering that simple fact will help you stay out of the performance realm and in the worship realm. Always remember you're doing it for Him.

Dancing

You have turned for me my mourning into dancing;
   you have loosed my sackcloth
   and clothed me with gladness,
that my glory may sing your praise and not be silent.
   O Lord my God, I will give thanks to you forever!
   - Psalm 30:11, 12

If you thought people were self-conscious when it comes to lifting their hands in church, that's nothing compared to how they feel about dancing. Unless you come from a cultural background where dancing in church is a normal thing, it can be very difficult to make yourself dance before the Lord. Why is that? Because in the back of your head you can't stop thinking, "Everyone is going to be looking at me, and what will they think if I look ridiculous?"

It doesn't help that dancing is considered a worldly affectation by many in the church. We must remember that Satan didn't come up with singing, playing instruments or

How To Worship

dancing. Satan isn't a creator. He can only corrupt the perfection that God has already created. Music and dancing were God's idea, and the wicked versions we see in the world today are corruptions of God's original plan. Just because there are worldly singers and musicians, that doesn't mean we should forgo singing and music in church, does it? The same holds true when it comes to dancing.

Then how do we deal with the feeling that "everyone is looking at me!" Notice in verse 11 above that one of the things dancing does is loose you. If you're standing up in church supposedly worshiping God, but inside you're self-conscious about what people are thinking about you, then you aren't God-conscious because you can't be both at the same time. Dancing forces you to let go of the pride of self-consciousness, and in doing so you will find that you're able to experience greater freedom in worship.

When King David brought the Ark of the Covenant back to Jerusalem, he got so excited that he *"...danced before the Lord with all his might"* (II Samuel 6:14). Later his wife, Michal, was very critical of David. Her pride was embarrassed because David had danced with such abandon. What if David had cared more about what she thought then what God thought of him? Would God have been able to use him in as great a way throughout his life?

Everybody can dance. Maybe you're not ready to perform on stage, but everyone can dance. It might be easier to start during your private worship at home where no one can see you, then gradually ease into it during corporate worship. Even if your dance starts out as a little two-step shuffle side to side, just go for it. Do something. Start somewhere. I promise you that God will be pleased.

Bowing Down

> **But I, through the abundance**
> **of your steadfast love,**
> **will enter your house.**
> **I will bow down toward your holy temple**
> **in the fear of you. - Psalm 5:7**

The final posture of worship is bowing down before the Lord in reverence. When someone in church is about to lead us in prayer, we'll often hear him ask, "Please bow your heads in prayer." It's interesting to me that nowhere in the Bible does it ever mention bowing your head in prayer. In fact, when Jesus prayed in John chapter 17, the Bible says, *"... he lifted up his eyes to heaven, and said..."* (John 17:1).

However, there are many Scripture verses about bowing down or kneeling in reverence before the Lord. There are times in worship when the presence of God becomes overwhelming, and you feel as though you can barely stand in His glory. It's not uncommon during times like this to see people kneeling on their hands and knees, or even lying prostrate on the floor before the Lord.

You shouldn't do anything in worship just because you see others around you doing it. Don't feel like you have to bow, but if you feel like you want to then go ahead and do it. Similar to lifting your hands, bowing in worship is a way of showing God you are completely submitted to Him.

How To Worship

Reflections of the Heart

Out of all the peoples of the world that He could've chosen to represent His name, God chose the Israelites. Why did He do that? I believe it was because they were such a very expressive people.

When they were sad, they wailed and tore their clothes and threw dirt in their hair. When they were happy, they danced and shouted and everyone around them knew they were happy. God wanted a people who would be outwardly demonstrative when they worshiped Him, and He still wants that today.

Every one of these physical postures of worship (standing, clapping, lifting holy hands, bowing down) are outward expressions of something that's happening on the inside. Standing shows respect, alertness and expectation. Clapping indicates victorious excitement. These actions of the body are outward reflections of the inward heart.

When you lift your hands, the Bible says to do it *"...without wrath and doubting"* (I Timothy 2:8). You shouldn't be angry inside about surrendering to God, and you shouldn't have doubt in your heart as you reach up to receive from Him. Likewise, bowing shows a deep inward respect and reverence for the Lord.

Of course you can go through all these motions outwardly and your heart still be far from God. The Pharisees did it in Jesus' day and some still do it every Sunday morning. You can deceive all the people around you, but you can't fool Him. So why bother trying?

The Outer Court

Summary

Entering the Temple to worship under the Old Covenant meant starting at the Outer Court. The Outer Court was mainly where thanksgiving, the first phase of worship, took place. Today under the New Covenant, when you go to your temple to worship you still have to start with the Outer Court: your body.

As with anything else, the more you practice the better you'll get, so practice worshiping. You'll find as you become more proficient in worship that your confidence will increase, and entering the Outer Court will become easier. We all tend to get more enjoyment from those things we feel that we're good at.

Sometimes when you get started worshiping, you won't feel like you're into it at first. You have to make a sacrifice of praise to get things going. The Outer Court included the Bronze Altar, which was where the daily sacrifices were performed. Jesus' sacrifice on the cross has made all other animal sacrifices unnecessary and redundant, but there is a sacrifice we're still told to bring:

Offer to God a sacrifice of thanksgiving, and perform your vows to the Most High.
  - Psalm 50:14

With increased confidence you'll eventually desire to worship God even more, and the Sunday morning experience will no longer be enough to completely satisfy you. You'll find yourself making space in your weekly schedule for worship, making it more of a priority,

How To Worship

because you'll want to spend more time in the presence of God.

The Outer Court was also where the Laver was found. This was where the priests of the Temple washed to cleanse themselves. Today Jesus our High Priest cleanses us *"...by the washing of water with the word."* (Ephesians 5:26). One thing all good praise and worship music has in common is it's full of the Word of God.

This corresponds to the Laver in the New Testament temple. By "washing" in the Word contained in those songs, the believer is able to scrape away the mire and contamination of the world while in the Outer Court, and once sanctified, is then prepared to proceed into the Inner Court.

Chapter 4 Discussion Questions

1. If your body is the literal temple of God, what does it mean to deliver your physical body to a place of worship? Why is it necessary?

2. If worship is primarily a spiritual experience, then why does it matter how we engage our bodies during worship?

3. What is the Audience Principle? How does an understanding of that principle help us in praise and worship?

4. Praise and worship is usually led by a talented worship leader. Why do you think God trusted them with that position? What preparation do they have to go through before a service? Do they have any more rights or privileges before God than other members of the congregation?

5. What happens if you worry more about what people might think of your outward expressions of worship than about what God thinks of you? What are some ways we can overcome our own self-consciousness during worship?

6. Does thanksgiving always have to be done out loud? What is the benefit of audible thanksgiving? Who else benefits when your thanksgiving can be heard?

Chapter 5

The Inner Court
Perfect Praise

... Hallelujah!
For our Lord God Almighty reigns.
Let us rejoice and be glad
and give him glory! - Revelation 19:6, 7

    About halfway through the song service your joy finally started coming back. Praise God, you were able to shake off the frustrations from earlier in the morning, and now you're clapping and swaying with the music and really enjoying the praise team's singing. Hey, there's Sister Susie. You need to talk with her about this week's home Bible study group. There's Brother Jim behind her, boy he's lost a lot of weight! Here comes Pastor into the sanctuary. What's he wearing today? You wonder what he's going to talk about in his sermon. Oh and there's Brother John, you need to talk to him about the church picnic. That reminds you that you need to stop by the grocery store on the way home to pick up a couple of things. Let's see, milk, bread, wait, what are they singing now? Some new song they're trying out. You don't really care for it much, plus you just heard someone play a wrong note. The worship team is pretty good but it sure would be nice if they'd learn to focus a little bit more.

How To Worship

Leaving the Outer Court of the New Covenant temple, you now step into the Inner Court. The Inner Court represents your soul, which consists of your mind, will and emotions. After getting your body in line in the Outer Court, you next have to begin focusing on your "soul realm." In the Outer Court thanksgiving is the primary mode of worship, but in the Inner Court that shifts over to praise.

Soul Control

Bless the Lord, O my soul;
And all that is within me, bless His holy name!
Bless the Lord, O my soul,
And forget not all His benefits:
Who forgives all your iniquities,
Who heals all your diseases,
Who redeems your life from destruction,
Who crowns you with lovingkindness and
    tender mercies,
Who satisfies your mouth with good things,
So that your youth is renewed like the eagle's.
    - Psalm 103:1-5

One of the secret keys to spiritual growth is developing your ability to concentrate. It can help you stay focused in the midst of distractions and keep you from missing valuable revelations from God. When it comes to your soul, you'll need to concentrate your mind so your thoughts don't wander, and set your will to praise Him so He can minister to your emotions by the Holy Spirit.

Let me give you an example: you're in church on

The Inner Court

Sunday listening to a message, and a baby starts crying in the back somewhere. The minister continues to speak, but the person beside you is distracted and looks back, missing what's being said. You, on the other hand, have learned to focus your mind, so you get a nugget of insight from his words and it answers a question you've been wrestling with for weeks. What if you had been distracted for a moment and missed that?

Jesus said, *"By your patience possess your souls"* (Luke 21:19). This isn't something that happens overnight. It's something you work at and develop toward. It may take you awhile, but stick with it until your soul is brought under your control. Notice in Psalm 103, quoted above, that the psalmist isn't speaking to God. He's talking to his own soul. He's focusing his soul – his mind, will and emotions – on the Lord.

Paraphrasing, the Psalmist is saying, *"Bless the Lord, oh my soul, and all that is within me bless His holy name! Don't forget what He's done for you, how He forgave you, how He healed you, how He spared you from destruction, how He lovingly provides for you and how He strengthens you."* Do you see how he's training his soul to focus on the Lord?

This is what you have to start doing in the Inner Court of your temple. It's not possible to do this through natural will power alone, but it can be done through the power of praise. Praise is a spiritual force that will literally bring the power of God down from Heaven and into your life. Praising God will empower you to bring your soul under control and equip you to enter the Most Holy Place.

How To Worship

Seven Hebrew Words for Praise

In order to better understand how praise can do this, let's look to the Scriptures. The Old Testament was originally written in Hebrew, and there are seven distinct words in the Hebrew language for praise. To gain more insight into the power of praise, let us now examine each one individually.

Yadah

So I will bless you as long as I live; in your name I will *(yadah)* lift up my hands. – Psalm 63:5

Yad is a verb that means "to use the extended hand, to throw out the open hand in a direction (as though throwing a stone)." and therefore *yadah* means "to worship God with extended hand." We covered lifting your hands as a physical posture of worship in the last chapter, but there's more to it than that.

When you *yadah,* you throw your hands up with strength and force, as though you were throwing something into the air. It also carries the connotation of a young child throwing his arms up to be picked up by his mother. The opposite meaning is "to bemoan, with the wringing of the hands."

Yadah is also a gesture of victory. To help you understand this better, think about when a touchdown is scored in football. The official lifts his two arms in the air as the regulation symbol that a touchdown has been scored, but he isn't excited about it. On the other hand, the fans also make the same touchdown symbol with their arms, but they throw their arms in the air with great excitement.

When King Jehoshaphat went into battle against three enemy nations, he had his praise team lead the army. This wasn't a great military strategy, but it was an excellent spiritual strategy. As they praised, the three enemy armies attacked each other and they were all destroyed. The Hebrew word translated as "praise" throughout that passage is *yadah* (II Chronicles 20:19-23).

Lifting your hands in praise isn't just a charismatic thing, it's a Bible thing, and it's always associated with victory through God. Our hands are an extension of our inner nature. To *yadah* is not just to lift your hands in a lazy, lackluster way, but to do so victoriously and enthusiastically. When you *yadah*, the enemy will flee.

Towdah

Whoever offers praise *(towdah)* glorifies me; And to him who orders his conduct aright, I will show the salvation of God. - Psalm 50:23

Towdah comes from the same principle root word as *yadah*, but it has a more specific meaning. It means to extend the hands and declare openly, freely, and unreservedly. Note the scripture above says *"Whoever offers..."* This is the kind of praise related to the sacrifice of praise we mentioned previously (Hebrews 13:15).

It also means "to say the same thing," and has the connotation of confession. When you *towdah*, it

How To Worship

affects your manner of life by helping you to order your conduct aright. To *towdah* is to work out your own salvation. While the *yadah* praise was directed entirely toward God because He alone gives us victory, the *towdah* praise is not only for God's benefit, but also for the benefit of our fellow believers.

The title of Psalm 100 is, *"A Psalm of Praise (towdah)"*, and the word appears again in verse 4: *"Enter into His gates with thanksgiving (towdah)..."* By using towdah in the title, the author is saying, "This is a psalm that we're all going to say together." The idea conveyed is that of a choir all singing the same words in unison.

Picture a group of believers with their right hands raised as though they were swearing an oath together and you'll have an idea of what *towdah* looks like – hands extended, all speaking the same thing by faith. When you *towdah,* you're thanking God for the things you've received by faith and also for those things you haven't received yet, and you're doing it where your Christian brothers and sisters can see you so that their faith can be strengthened as well. This is what happened in the Book of Acts.

When the early church was forbidden to speak in the Name of Jesus, the Bible says *"...when they heard that, <u>they raised their voice to God with one accord and said</u>: 'Lord, You are God, who made heaven and earth and the sea and all that is in them...'"* (Acts 4:24). They made a unified confession of faith. When the minister says, "Everybody say Praise the Lord," and then everyone in the congregation in unison replies, "Praise the Lord," that is an example of *towdah* praise.

Halal

Praise *(halal)* the Lord! *(Jah)*
Praise *(halal)*, O servants of the Lord, *(Jah)*
Praise *(halal)* the name of the Lord! *(Jah)*
Blessed be the name of the Lord
From this time forth and forevermore!
From the rising of the sun to its going down
The Lord's name is to be praised *(halal).*
  - Psalm 113:1-3

Halal is the root Hebrew word from which we derive the word "Hallelujah," a universal word for praise in every language of the world. It's composed of two Hebrew words, *halal* and *Jah*, an abbreviation of *Jehovah*, which is one of the names of God: *Halal+Jah* = Hallelujah.

Halal means "to be clear, to shine, to boast, show, to rave, celebrate, to be clamorously foolish." To *halal* is to boast in the Lord. It denotes meeting together and telling of His greatness. This isn't so much a demonstration like raising your hands or dancing, but rather talking about His awesome greatness.

Notice the repetitiveness in Psalm 113 (quoted above). *Halal* indicates a kind of praise that we should be making over and over again. Never stop telling of His greatness, never stop telling of His victories and never stop telling of His great love for us. Hallelujah! The *halal* praise is a great way to encourage yourself in the Lord, along with all of the people around you.

How To Worship

Halal praising isn't just about boasting in the Lord's victories. It's also something that should get us worked up. To *halal* means more than just talking about it. It's going beyond that until you're clamorously foolish. It's celebrating and raving about the greatness of God. Sometimes Pentecostals are questioned about their demonstrative worship, but we Spirit-filled Christians have a long way to go to catch up to the ancient Israelites.

Following Psalm 113, Psalm 114 is a great example of this type of raving praise. Remember, these were songs God's people sang. Think of what a pitiful group the nation of Israel was as Moses led them out of Egypt: a bunch of recently freed slaves who were running for their lives. Yet their focus wasn't on their problems or the things they lacked. In Psalm 114 their *halal* was centered only on the greatness of God.

Psalms 113 and 114 were sung by the Israelites just prior to the Passover meal. That means, at the Last Supper, on the night before He would die on the cross, Jesus and His disciples were *halal*-ing God. Our Lord used this form of praise to encourage Himself and His men, and to gird them up for the challenges that were just hours away. If Jesus hadn't *halal* praised in the upper room, would He have been able to pray through at Gethsemane, I wonder?

How much more then do we as believers need to *halal* the Lord for our own encouragement? We should be talking about Him constantly, lifting up His name, magnifying His greatness, *"from the rising of the sun to its going down..."* As Christians, *halal* praising should become second nature to us. It should become something you do without even having to think about it.

Shabach

Praise the Lord, all you Gentiles!
Laud *(shabach)* Him, all you peoples!
For His merciful kindness is great toward us,
And the truth of the Lord endures forever.
  - Psalm 117:1

Shabach means, "to shout, to address in a loud tone, to command, to triumph." Many Christians today consider shouting in church to be more of a cultural tradition that some churches follow and others do not, but the reality is that shouting praises to God is Biblical and not a man-made tradition at all.

The enemy tries to discourage us from shouting praises unto God. His is the voice in your head that says, *"Shouldn't you tone it down a little bit? You don't want to make a fool of yourself, do you?"* Satan wants to belittle and embarrass us for shouting because he fears the spiritual power that is released when we *shabach* in faith.

Psalm 63 was written while David was being hunted by King Saul. He was running for his life, hiding in caves, hungry, thirsty and exhausted. It was one of the lowest points in his life, but being who he was, David turned to the Lord in his trial and wrote a praise song about it. Look at how this psalm begins:

O God, You are my God;
Early will I seek You;

How To Worship

> **My soul thirsts for You;**
> **My flesh longs for You**
> **In a dry and thirsty land**
> **Where there is no water.**
> **So I have looked for You in the sanctuary,**
> **To see Your power and Your glory.**
> **Because Your lovingkindness is better than life,**
> **My lips shall praise *(shabach)* You.**
> **– Psalm 63:1-3 (NKJ)**

That last line could be more literally translated, *"My lips shall SHOUT unto You."* In the midst of one of the most difficult seasons of his life, David didn't come out with a quiet whisper of praise. David shouted his praise to God. He wasn't worried about getting too loud. He didn't concern himself with what people would think about him. Far more important than that to David was the fact that he had to get out of this situation he was in, and he did that by *shabach*-ing to the Lord.

A *shabach* praise isn't just a loud shout for the sake of being loud. It's a triumphant shout. It's the war cry of the soldier as he's about to descend into battle against his enemies. He may be outmanned and outgunned in the natural, but his *shabach* of praise terrifies his opponents as he charges toward them, and that brings him the victory. There may be times when you feel overwhelmed by the circumstances of life and your temptation will be to retreat in fear. Instead you must *shabach* at those circumstances.

Finally, to *shabach* is to shout not only in praise, not only in triumph, but also to shout out in faith. It's a shout of command and authority, ordering adverse circumstances to line up with the Word of God. The best example of this in the Bible is when Jesus spoke to the storm, *"Peace, be still!"* (Mark 4:35-41). The *shabach* is the command of faith that will still all the storms in your life.

Barak

Oh come, let us worship and bow down;
let us kneel *(barak)* before the Lord, our Maker!
   - Psalm 95:6

Barak means "to kneel down, to bless God as an act of adoration." All of the Hebrew words for praise we've covered so far have been very physically demonstrative, but *barak* praise involves a deep moving of the Spirit on your heart where you just want to linger in this holy moment of reverential awe.

Chronologically, Psalm 72 was the last psalm King David wrote (see Psalm 72:20). He wrote this song reflecting on a long life of God's faithfulness toward him, despite David's numerous flaws and mistakes. He recognized his utter dependence on God every day of his life in a *barak* praise:

He will redeem their life from oppression and violence;
And precious shall be their blood in His sight.
And He shall live;
And the gold of Sheba will be given to Him;
Prayer also will be made for Him continually,
And daily He shall be praised *(barak)*.
   - Psalm 72:14, 15

Kneeling in *barak* praise doesn't convey an attitude of begging. You aren't on your knees because of a feeling of shame or unworthiness, but rather you're kneeling with a sense of expectation, overwhelmed by the power and might of God to overcome all of your problems.

There are times when we need to get quiet and let His presence wash over us, to be still and know that He is God (Psalm 46:10). We Spirit-filled believers love to come before the Lord with lively worship, loud music and shouting, but this *barak* type of praise is just as important in our lives, and it's no less spiritual than the other types of praise.

Tehillah

Praise the Lord!
Sing *(tehillah)* to the Lord a new song,
his praise in the assembly of the godly!
   - Psalm 149:1

Tehillah also comes from the word *halal*. It is defined as "the singing of *halals*, to sing or to laud; perceived to involve music, especially singing; hymns of the Spirit." Obviously, it's very common for singing to be involved with praise.

Singing is a very popular method of praise in the Kingdom of God, both in Heaven and on the Earth. It can be found in both the Old and New Testaments, and in every church no matter what the denomination. It's an activity that is not limited to just God's people. Angels

The Inner Court

sing together (Job 38:7), and even God Himself rejoices over us *"...with loud singing."* (Zephaniah 3:17).

The fact is if you don't learn how to worship with singing, when you get to Heaven you're going to be the odd man out. Many people (many, many people) will respond by saying, "But I can't sing." That simply isn't true.

Everybody can *tehillah*. Some can sing better than others, but everyone can sing. I would characterize myself as an above-average singer. I'm not a great singer, or even a good one, but I'm not a bad singer either. I will never record an album, but I can sing. And so can you.

Now let me be very blunt here. I said everyone (including you) can sing. That is absolutely 100% true. However, not everyone needs to sing into a microphone, and not everyone should record. Everyone can sing, but not everyone needs to be heard. However, even if your singing sounds like a donkey braying in a tin barn at midnight, you can still sing to God.

If you truly are a poor singer, you really should sing anyway. If you're worshiping at home, alone, no one is going to hear except you and God, and He will be pleased with your singing, even if you think it's technically lacking. If you're in a congregation full of people, sing just loud enough that you can hear yourself, but not so loud that you cannot hear the instruments playing and those singing around you.

In other words, don't sing so loud you throw them off, but still sing because it's something you're doing for the Lord, not for them. "I can't sing" is a lie. He is your audience, and He will enjoy it.

Zamar

**Let them praise His name with the dance;
Let them sing praises *(zamar)* to Him with the timbrel and harp. - Psalm 149:3**

Zamar means "to pluck the strings of an instrument, to sing, to praise; a musical word which is largely involved with joyful expressions of music with musical instruments. Playing musical instruments is another form of praise that almost everyone can do. Obviously, not nearly so many people are skilled instrumentalists as they are singers, but even people with no musical training can play along with the praise band using a tambourine or some similar instrument.

If you are a musician, you know that you have to practice to keep your skill level high. Worshiping with your instrument when you're alone is a great way to experience intimate time with the Almighty, and it can make practice time a lot less of a drudgery too. Whether we are singing or playing an instrument, we need to always remember the Audience Principle of worship, that is, Who the principle audience really is.

When an evil spirit troubled King Saul, his servants sought out "... *a man who is skillful in playing the lyre, and when the harmful spirit from God is upon you, he will play it, and you will be well.*" (I Samuel 16:16). They found a young shepherd boy named David, and when "*...David took the lyre and played it with his hand. So Saul was refreshed and was well, and the harmful spirit departed from him.*"

The Inner Court

(I Samuel 16:23). When anointed music is present, tormenting spirits cannot remain.

Music stirs the anointing. This is a point that applies to singing as well as *zamar*-ing. The Bible says God inhabits and dwells in the praises of His people (Psalm 22:3). The anointing isn't an impersonal force; He's a Person. It's a recognizable manifestation of the God who is always there, yet it is at that moment He is making His presence known by His Spirit and felt in a tangible way. Music isn't required to worship, but don't fail to take advantage of anointed music whenever you have the opportunity to do so.

At the same time, it's worth noting that of the seven Hebrew words for praise, only two of them, *tehillah* and *zamar*, are directly related to music. When it comes to worship, anointed music played skillfully can be an enormous help to get you into a place of praise, but it's not a requirement. You should practice praising God without music sometimes. There may come a time when the music isn't there, but that doesn't mean you can't praise Him.

Summary

Numbers have symbolic meaning in the Bible, and seven is considered to be God's number because it's the number that typifies completeness and perfection. It's not a coincidence that there are seven Hebrew words that are translated "praise" in our English Bible, because God wants our praise to be perfect.

The word "perfection" in the Bible doesn't mean

How To Worship

what we normally think of as perfect, meaning flawless or without mistakes. We all know we'll never be without mistakes in this life, and yet Jesus commanded that *"You therefore must be perfect, as your heavenly Father is perfect"* (Matthew 5:48). How could we ever be able to obey this command? It becomes possible when we understand that the Old English word "perfection" actually means "completeness" or "maturity."

The furniture of the Old Testament Temple's Inner Court illustrates this goal. The Table of Shewbread represents our fellowship with Him. The oil-burning Lampstand represents the illumination of the Holy Spirit that comes to us during times of praise. Finally, the Altar of Incense represents the change in atmosphere that the anointing brings as our purest prayers ascend to the throne of God in the form of praise.

The Inner Court, also called the Holy Place, is where you practice praising. It's the place where your praise becomes complete and mature. At the Outer Court you bring your body into God's presence with thanksgiving. Here in the Inner Court, you center your soul on worshiping the Lord with praise, and as you do so you're able to filter out mental distractions and focus your thoughts exclusively on Him.

Once you've passed through the Outer Court and the Inner Court of your New Testament temple, you're now ready to enter the Most Holy Place, the Holy of Holies.

Chapter 5 Discussion Questions

1. In light of Luke 21:19, discuss the value of mental focus during praise and worship.

2. Why do you have to encourage your soul sometimes like David in Psalm 103? How does praise help you do that?

3. How is the Hebrew word *halal* similar to a coach's pep talk at half-time? How is it different?

4. How does knowing the seven types of praise help you to praise God? Can you use them intentionally? How does it help to focus and refine your thoughts during worship?

5. If you watch someone else work out, does your body receive any benefit? If you simply sit and watch a praise and worship team perform, what benefit do you gain from that? How many ways can you participate in praise and worship without any music?

6. How does it help you to understand that when the Bible speaks about "perfection," the actual meaning is "completeness" or "maturity"? How does it help you in praise and worship? How might it help in other areas of your life?

7. Try this as a personal spiritual exercise: the next time you find yourself praising God, take a moment to identify which type of praise you just made: *yadah, towdah, halal, shabach, barak, tehillah* or *zamar?* Think back to the last moment you praised God recently. Which type of praise was it?

Chapter 6

The Most Holy Place
Psalms, Hymns and Spiritual Songs

Therefore do not be unwise, but understand what the will of the Lord is. And do not be drunk with wine, in which is dissipation; but be filled with the Spirit, speaking to one another in psalms and hymns and spiritual songs, singing and making melody in your heart to the Lord, giving thanks always for all things to God the Father in the name of our Lord Jesus Christ, submitting to one another in the fear of God.
  – Ephesians 5:17-21 (NKJ)

The frustrations of the morning are now a distant memory as your body is fully in sync with worshiping God. The various mental distractions moments ago have been replaced with a keen focus on the awe inspiring presence of God. You've entered His gates with thanksgiving as the praise team's fast songs have carried you through the Outer Court. You've entered His courts with praise as the slightly slower music has carried you through the Inner Court. Now you stand at the entrance to the Holy of Holies where the very presence of God dwells, ready to enter with your worship. Eyes closed, hands raised, thoughts centered,

How To Worship

This... this moment right here in His presence... this is why you worship the way you do.

Welcome to the Most Holy Place of the New Covenant temple. As the Outer Court represents the body or the "flesh realm," and the Inner Court represents the inward thoughts or the "soul realm," so the Holy of Holies represents the real you, your spirit-man. Your spirit is the part of you that will live forever, either in Heaven or in Hell. It's the part of you that was recreated when you first believed and confessed Jesus Christ as your Lord (II Corinthians 5:17).

The real you isn't your body, because when you die the real you won't be inside that body any longer (II Corinthians 5:8). The real you isn't your soul, because the soul is what was created between the spirit and body when God first breathed life into Adam's body (Genesis 2:7). The real you is your spirit, and Jesus said God is also a Spirit, and those who worship Him must do so in spirit and in truth (John 4:24).

Notice in Ephesians 5:17, quoted above, that Paul gives instruction to "*... not be unwise, but understand what the will of the Lord is.*" Although this book has covered the subject of how to worship in depth, worship is actually very simple. Theological training is required to complicate it. Paul goes on to describe Spirit-filled worship: "speaking to one another in psalms and hymns and spiritual songs, singing and making melody in your heart to the Lord."

These three methods of worship, speaking in psalms, hymns, and spiritual songs, all take place

78

The Most Holy Place

within the Holy of Holies of your New Testament temple, your spirit, the place where the presence of God resides within you. According to Paul, all three of these are evidence of the Spirit-filled believer. If that's the case, then we need to learn what the Bible means when it instructs us to sing in psalms, hymns and spiritual songs from our spirit. Otherwise, how can we obey this command if we don't even know what these three things are? Let's examine these three methods of spiritual worship so that we can.

Psalms

Psalms are defined as songs of praise from Scripture, or songs that are in the character, spirit, or manner of the Old Testament psalms. The function of psalms is that they are primarily directed toward God. Obviously, the Book of Psalms is our primary source material when it comes to studying psalms, but that isn't the only place psalms can be found in the Bible.

The Song of Moses and Miriam (Exodus 15:1-21), sung immediately following the deliverance of the children of Israel from the Egyptians at the Red Sea, is one example of a psalm located elsewhere in the Bible. The Song of David (II Samuel 22), celebrating David's deliverance from the hand of Saul and all of his other enemies is another example.

Today the Book of Psalms is located alongside the other books of poetry in the Bible, so it can be easy for us to forget that it was originally a song book. In fact, many modern Bible translations, such as the English Standard Version (ESV) include the translation from the Hebrew of

How To Worship

the musical direction preceding each Psalm, instructing how they are to be played.

If you read through the Book of Psalms carefully in a translation that includes them, you will see these musical directions. For example, prior to verse 1, Psalm 4 says, *"To the choirmaster: with stringed instruments. A Psalm of David."* The point is you need to retrain yourself to recognize the Psalms as not just chapters and verses, but as the musical compositions they originally were.

Another characteristic of psalms is they are very raw. When David was down and feeling like everything around him was falling apart, he'd write a song along the lines of, "Hey God, I'm feeling really down and everything around me is falling apart. Where are you anyway?" We live in a fallen world where life isn't always sweetness and light, and psalms reflect that fact.

There's a great lesson in the Psalms when it comes to being honest with God. There are times when we can really relate to how David felt on his down days, but we try to hide those feelings from the people around us. It might be pride or it might be that we're standing in faith and don't want to say or do anything that will contradict the promise we're standing on. Whatever the case, God still knows the thoughts and intent of our heart.

You might fool everyone around you successfully, but you'll never fool God. He knows, so you might as well be honest with Him. Always be brutally honest with yourself, and always be brutally honest with the Lord. If

The Most Holy Place

you're angry or sad or devastated, don't try to pretend like you're not. Instead take your anger, sadness and despair to Him and let Him minister to you.

How do we "sing" psalms? If we wanted to obey Paul's instruction in Ephesians 5:18, what would that look like? Firstly, there are some Christian musicians who have set some of the Psalms to music. These are modern songs that take a Psalm, set it to music, and sing it word for word. Keith Green's rendition of Psalm 23 is extremely moving. *Sons of Korah* is a group whose entire body of work is various Psalms set to music, and there are many others.

Beyond songs like that, another way to sing Psalms is simply to open the Book of Psalms, look at the words, and start singing them. You say, "But I don't know the tune of the Psalm. I don't know how it's supposed to go." Of course you don't. No one does, but so what? Do you want to obey or don't you? I'm being completely serious here.

There are many times I've turned to a favorite Psalm and sung it as a form of worship toward the Lord. I've never done it from the platform at church because I'm not a great singer. In fact, I'm fairly certain that some of the Psalms I've sung to the Lord haven't come out the same way twice, but my musical proficiency isn't the point.

The point is I'm a Spirit-filled believer, and I want to worship God in truth and please Him by doing what He says. One of the ways I can do that is to sing Psalms to Him. How about you? If you've never psalmed before, I encourage you to try it.

How To Worship

Hymns

Hymns are defined as songs of praise that are original human compositions, containing an element of praise but going beyond praise to address various divine themes. Hymns teach man about God's actions, His character, and His purposes. They are intended to provoke man into further response toward God.

Church hymnals are our primary source for hymns, and they include many songs you've probably heard before. The New Testament was originally written in Greek, and the Greek word for hymns is *humneo*. Quoting Psalm 22, the author of Hebrews says:

> **saying, "I will tell of your name to my brothers; in the midst of the congregation I will sing your praise *(humneo)*." - Hebrews 2:12**

Hymns are praise songs that are testimonial or glorifying to God, but they are directed primarily towards man. In contrast, psalms intend for God to be the primary and exclusive recipient of the song.

Examples include *Amazing Grace, There Is A Fountain Filled With Blood*, and *Just As I Am* among many, many others. Hymns are considered old-fashioned or out of style by many people today, but this only demonstrates that the spiritual power contained in these songs is not fully understood in our day.

One characteristic of a true hymn is it's packed full

of the Word of God. Every verse and refrain contains references to Holy Scripture. Hymns have so much Bible in them that many of them could literally be called sermons within a song. To say that hymns have gone out of style would be as foolish as saying the Word of God has gone out of style.

Because hymns are so full of the Word, the verses of a hymn can be "preached" like a sermon if they are spoken without the music. This is another characteristic of a true hymn. Consider some of the words from the hymns mentioned above. This example works better when you can hear someone saying it out loud, but try to imagine these words being preached from the pulpit on Sunday morning by a fiery Holy Ghost preacher:

<u>Amazing Grace</u> - by John Newton

Amazing grace! How sweet the sound
That saved a wretch like me.
I once was lost, but now am found,
Was blind, but now I see.

Through many dangers, toils and snares
I have already come;
'Tis grace hath brought me safe thus far
And grace will lead me home.

When we've been there ten thousand years
Bright shining as the sun,
We've no less days to sing God's praise
Than when we've first begun.

How To Worship

<u>There Is A Fountain</u> - by William Cowper

*There is a fountain filled with blood,
Drawn from Immanuel's veins,
And sinners plunged beneath that flood
Lose all their guilty stains.*

<u>Just As I Am</u> – Charlotte Elliott

*Just as I am, without one plea,
but that thy blood was shed for me,
and that thou bidst me come to thee,
O Lamb of God, I come, I come.*

One thing we need to always remember with hymns, however, is that they are of human composition. The lyrics of hymns are not Holy Spirit inspired in the same sense as the words of the Book of Psalms. That means we have to be careful when using them in worship. Most hymns are excellent, but we always need to make sure what we're singing agrees with Scripture.

Hymns have largely fallen out of favor today, having been replaced for the most part by simple praise choruses. However, because they are based on the timeless Word of God, some of them have been making a quiet comeback, with their music slightly altered to match up with contemporary styles. You should make an effort to learn some hymns if you haven't been exposed to them very much in your own Christian experience.

All hymnals are written in four-part harmony, so if you can read music it's not hard to learn the melody of a hymn. If you don't read music, you can still find many collections of hymns on compact disc and you can learn them that way. There are also many websites that contain hymn lyrics, and several of those web sites will also allow you to play the hymn so you can hear its tune.

I strongly believe one of the main reasons hymns have supposedly "gone out of style" is that Satan recognizes and fears the spiritual power they contain. Don't make the mistake of missing out on the blessing of worshiping God through the singing of hymns just because it's popular today to call them old-fashioned.

The Apostle Paul knew a little something about the power of God, and he said we should sing hymns. Paul and Silas experienced the power of singing hymns late one night in a Philippian jail cell right before an earthquake freed them:

About midnight Paul and Silas were praying and singing hymns to God, and the prisoners were listening to them, - Acts 16:25

An example in the New Testament is Zacharias' Benedictus in Luke 1:68-79. Paul's letters also included passages that followed the pattern of hymns, such as Philippians 2:6-11, Colossians 1:15-20 and I Timothy 3:16. One can easily see the doctrinal teaching contained in those passages, which is one of the main functions of a hymn.

In Matthew 26:30 we read what happened at the

Last Supper immediately after Jesus concluded His remarks to the disciples: *"And when they had sung a hymn, they went out to the Mount of Olives."* If singing hymns was good enough for Jesus, the Twelve, and Paul, then it should be good enough for you.

Spiritual Songs

Spiritual songs are defined as prophetic songs of a spontaneous and unpremeditated nature, with unrehearsed melodies, sung under the impetus of the Holy Spirit. Many denominational churches allow only the singing of hymns in their services. Other churches have introduced psalms and scriptural choruses, but there is a great reluctance to allow the functioning of spiritual songs, even though the Bible groups all three of them together.

I've been blessed to participate in services where there were musicians who were able to move proficiently in spiritual songs. When the minister finished his message, he'd look over to these musicians and ask them, "Do you have anything?" What he meant was, "Has the Holy Spirit given you a spiritual song?" Many times they would have something.

The musician would walk to the piano and begin playing and singing a song that was brand new, one that no one had ever heard before, and yet it was scriptural and related to the message that had just been spoken, concluding the message with victorious anointed worship. A person who didn't understand spiritual songs might think, "Wow, that guy is extremely talented to be able to come up with such a perfect song on the spot like that," not realizing that it was the Holy Spirit who had given it to him just moments before!

Most Christians aren't musicians who operate at that level with spiritual songs, yet we can still experience this form of worship. The opportunity most often comes toward the end of the worship part of the service, when the songs are slower and the worship of God is more intimate. When the worship team ends one song, sometimes they will pause before moving on to the next song, but the music will keep playing, and during that pause the worship leader will encourage the congregation to "sing your own song to the Lord" or something along those lines.

This is when you can start singing a spiritual song. These songs will always take one of two forms: either a prophetic inspired song sung in a known tongue, or a song sung in an unknown tongue. The Apostle Paul said, *"...I will sing with the spirit, and I will also sing with the understanding"* (I Corinthians 14:15). Singing in the spirit means singing in tongues. A believer is able to speak and sing in tongues after they've received the infilling of the Holy Spirit (also sometimes referred to as the baptism in the Holy Spirit).

Another term used to describe spiritual songs is prophetic songs. It's beyond the scope of this book to fully teach on the gift of prophecy, but it does need to be touched on briefly in order to describe spiritual songs completely. "Prophetic" doesn't mean just predicting the future or having to do with the end times. In fact, that's a very small subset of the realm of prophecy. Strictly defined, prophecy means Holy Spirit-inspired utterance in a known language.

When it comes to prophetic spiritual songs, it must be understood that these are spontaneous songs inspired by the Holy Spirit that are sung or played in a known language. For example, instead of singing in tongues during that lull between worship songs, you might find yourself singing Spirit-inspired words in English instead. It's easier to sing in tongues than it is to sing in your own language, because it takes less faith to speak in tongues than it does to prophesy.

Notice that prophetic spiritual songs are defined as songs that are sung or played in a known language. Music is a language, and a musician who's learned to flow with the Holy Spirit in the realm of spiritual songs can play his instrument prophetically. The Bible talks about musicians prophesying on their instruments:

> **...as soon as you come to the city, you will meet a group of prophets coming down from the high place with harp, tambourine, flute, and lyre before them, prophesying. - I Samuel 10:5**

> **Moreover David and the captains of the army separated for the service some of the sons of Asaph, of Heman, and of Jeduthun, who should prophesy with harps, stringed instruments, and cymbals... - I Chronicles 25:1**

Speaking or singing in tongues is a gift that's particular to the New Covenant, but prophetic speech

The Most Holy Place

(Spirit-inspired speech in a known language) can be found throughout the Bible in both the Old and New Testaments. Prophetic speech is expressed in spoken language as well as the "language" of music. You may not realize it, but many of the popular worship songs you enjoy today started out as a spiritual song that was then captured and remembered.

At this point it should be very obvious that even many supposedly Spirit-filled churches have barely begun to plumb the depths of what is available to us from God in the realm of prophetic worship through spiritual songs. For many reading these pages, this is the first time you've ever heard it explained anywhere. Let me encourage you to not be intimidated, and also to not over-think it.

Practice stepping out in spiritual songs at church during those pauses and musical interludes between worship songs. Don't worry about messing up or drawing unwanted attention to yourself. Just sing quietly under your breath where only you can hear it. Everyone around you will probably be so caught up in worship they won't even notice you anyway.

Of course, you should also get started in spiritual songs in the privacy of your home. Some of the most satisfying worship I've ever had has been times when I was home alone and could sing out loud without worrying about embarrassment or criticism. Whether at church or at home, make the effort to start experiencing spiritual songs in your own life. Just as it is with any other promise found in the Bible, it is the doer of the Word who will be blessed (James 1:22).

Summary

In the Old Testament Temple, the Holy of Holies contained the Ark of the Covenant. Positioned in the very center of the lid of that Ark, between the two golden cherubim, was the Mercy Seat where the presence and glory of God dwelled. Entering into the Most Holy Place in your New Testament temple means bringing your spirit into His holy presence through worship, in a spirit-to-Spirit encounter that the Old Covenant saints could only dream about.

Spirit-filled worship means worshiping God from your own spirit in psalms, hymns and spiritual songs. It's one thing for a preacher or teacher to tell you this is something you ought to do, but now you've been taught how to do it, or at least how to get started. Try to realize how precious this revelation is. Many believers live out their entire Christian lives never learning a hint of these truths. Esteem it highly, and more importantly don't be a hearer only, but be a doer of the Word.

So far, worshiping God in spirit and in truth, and the defining of thanksgiving, praise and worship have been covered. Additionally, the true New Testament temple has been identified by recognizing that it's not a building made of natural materials, but rather a spiritual building made up of all believers corporately, and your spirit, your soul and your body make up your temple of the Holy Spirit individually.

Thanksgiving in the Outer Court of the body, praise in the Inner Court of the soul, and finally worship in the

The Most Holy Place

Holy of Holies of your spirit have also been revealed. The remainder of this book on How to Worship will focus on identifying and explaining the benefits of doing all these things you've learned, and providing you with practical examples that you can follow as you venture out on your own journey toward becoming a worshiper in spirit and in truth.

Chapter 6 Discussion Questions

1. The Psalms were written thousands of years ago, and yet the modern-day Christian can easily relate to them. Why?

2. Did David compose the Psalms and then write them down, or do you think they were improvised works which were written down later? Is it okay to repeat praises we find in the scriptures or do they always need to be improvised to truly be "from the heart"?

3. When David sang his Psalms, they were emotional, passionate, and very "raw." Do you think he sang them publicly among the congregation, or reserved them for his private time with God?

4. Most hymns we hear today are traditional 4-part songs with 4 verses. What does a modern hymn sound like? Are they always sung by a choir wearing robes, or can they be a different style of music?

5. Some traditional hymns were born out of the composer's personal experience. Why might the composer's testimony add value to the hymn?

6. What did you learn from this chapter about spiritual songs that was new to you? How do you think a better understanding of spiritual songs will aid you in worship?

7. Now that you know more about psalms, hymns and spiritual songs, what are some ways you can apply this new information? How do you envision yourself stepping out more into psalms, hymns and spiritual songs in the future?

Chapter 7

Why Should We Do This?
Motivation for Worship

Let the word of Christ dwell in you richly in all wisdom; teaching and admonishing one another in psalms and hymns and spiritual songs, singing with grace in your hearts to the Lord.
  - Colossians 3:16

By this point you've already learned a lot about How To Worship. Not only have you received a lot of new information, but you've also learned many different ways to apply that new knowledge in your life. Hopefully, you've already taken advantage of this opportunity by trying out some of the suggestions that have been given to help you get started.

If you haven't yet begun practicing these new methods of praise and worship that have been covered so far, or you need more motivation to get started, this chapter is for you. In the Introduction I promised you this wasn't going to be just a book of theory or theology, but actual hands-on steps you could start putting into practice right away.

How To Worship

With that said, it's good to be aware of the benefits of worship so you can be on the lookout for them from the moment you get started.

There are numerous spiritual blessings the church gains when she worships in the manner taught by the Bible. Some of these benefits apply to the church corporately, while others apply more toward the individual believer. Understanding the things you and your church have to gain through worshiping God will motivate you to press in even further.

Corporate Benefits of Worship

There are benefits that come from worshiping God which benefit not just the individual Christian, but the church as a whole. It's not an exaggeration to say that if a church's worship can be transformed, then that entire church can be transformed. What are some of the benefits of corporate worship?

Change of Focus

Therefore, as you received Christ Jesus the Lord, so walk in him, rooted and built up in him and established in the faith, just as you were taught, abounding in thanksgiving. - Colossians 2:6-7

Just as worship will change the focus of an individual believer, so it will also correct the focus of a congregation. There are so many things that can distract and dilute the attention of a church from the things of God – financial concerns, strife and division, the list could go on and on.

Why Should We Do This?

By focusing on the problems instead of praising God, the church can become self-centered and proud. Worship redirects the church's attention back to God and off of the problems.

Some churches are so involved in spiritual warfare that their attention is focused more on the devil than on God. There is a place for fighting and resisting the devil, but paying too much attention to the devil isn't good. Praise is a powerful weapon the church can use against the devil while at the same time still keeping her focus on God.

During Jesus' triumphal entry into Jerusalem on Palm Sunday, He quoted Psalm 8:2 which says, *"Out of the mouth of babies and infants, you have established strength because of your foes, to still the enemy and the avenger."* When Jesus quoted this verse, He substituted the words *"perfected praise"* for *"established strength"* (Matthew 21:16). This is a tremendous revelation: praise equals spiritual strength. Scriptural praise and worship will always change the focus of any gathering of believers for the better.

Divine Encounters

God inhabits the praises of His people.
- Psalm 22:3

With the change of focus that worship brings, divine encounters become possible. Just as God's very presence inhabited between the cherubim of the Ark of the Covenant in the Old Testament Temple, so God dwells within the praises of His people inside the New Covenant Temple. Think about that for a moment: when we

How To Worship

worship God, He shows up.

We understand from a theological standpoint that God is omnipresent, meaning He is everywhere and aware of everything. Yet, we're not always aware of His presence, are we? The prophet Isaiah said, *"Truly, you are a God who hides himself, O God of Israel, the Savior"* (Isaiah 45:15). God does most of His work behind the scenes, not out in the open. Yet when we praise Him, He reveals Himself.

It's very important for us to be able to discern when God is moving during worship. When things start happening during the worship service, we need to recognize that it's the Holy Spirit manifesting Himself. That's why Paul wrote, *"Do not quench the Spirit"* (I Thessalonians 5:19). In this atmosphere lives are changed, people are healed, and bondages are broken.

Freedom

Now the Lord is the Spirit, and where the Spirit of the Lord is, there is freedom.
- II Corinthians 3:17

God wants His people to be free from the chains the enemy would try to bind us with. The Bible says, "...God anointed Jesus of Nazareth with the Holy Spirit and with power. He went about doing good and healing all who were oppressed by the devil, for God was with him" (Acts 10:38). There are few places you will find the kind of freedom that can be found in praise and worship.

Besides breaking free from the chains of the enemy,

sincere and authentic worship will also help you break free of the chains which have bound you. When the cares and concerns about what other people might think of you when you worship a certain way are eclipsed by your desire to serve and please the Lord, you will experience a freedom in your spirit that will spill over into every other area of your life.

Unity

Submitting yourselves one to another in the fear of God. - Ephesians 5:21 (NKJ)

It's hard to be angry with someone standing next to you while you both are worshiping at the Throne of God. Sometimes conflicts happen, even with good people trying to do the right thing. It's so easy to allow slights and misunderstandings to lead to offense and strife that will ultimately quench the Spirit. That's why one of Satan's main strategies is to get believers into strife with one another.

The Apostle James said, *"For where envying and strife is, there is confusion and every evil work"* James 3:16 (KJV), and the Apostle John wrote that *"Anyone who does not love does not know God, because God is love."* (I John 4:8) Since God is love, it's only natural that spending time in His presence will make you a more loving person.

When a congregation worships the Lord together, hearts are softened and forgiveness flows. People lose track of their own agendas and begin to prioritize His agenda instead, and in doing so they begin to walk in love with one another more. Notice in Ephesians 5:21 (quoted above) that this submission to one another happens only in an environment of reverence toward Him.

Anointing

Let the word of Christ dwell in you richly in all wisdom; teaching and admonishing one another in psalms and hymns and spiritual songs, singing with grace in your hearts to the Lord. - Colossians 3:16 (NKJ)

Psalm 133 compares unity to the anointing oil that was poured over Aaron, the High Priest. Oil is a symbol of the Holy Spirit, and anointing oil is a symbol of the anointing of the Holy Spirit. We already looked at Acts 10:38, *"How God anointed Jesus of Nazareth with the Holy Spirit and with power..."* The anointing is the power of God manifested in the Person of the Holy Spirit, and unity leads directly to the anointing.

The New Testament was originally written in Greek, and then translated into English much later. The word "grace" in Colossians 3:16 (quoted above) is a translation of the Greek word *charis,* from which we derive our word "charismatic" to describe Spirit-filled believers and churches. Another way to say a person is anointed to minister is to say they are graced to be able to do that. It means that it's evident that what the person is doing is not being done on his own, but with divine assistance.

Many people assume that being anointed to worship relates exclusively to the singers and musicians of the praise and worship team, but that is an incorrect assumption. When a congregation in unity sings before the Lord, they aren't just singing pretty notes. They're *"...singing with grace in their hearts..."* or in other words they are worshiping with anointed singing.

Individual Benefits

All of the benefits of corporate worship will bless the believer as an individual, but there are also spiritual benefits that are specific to individual worship. The advantage of these benefits is you can partake of them outside of your corporate worship setting. In other words, while you can receive these blessings on Sunday morning, you don't have to wait until then. There are benefits you can experience through individual worship in the privacy of your own home. These benefits are covered in the verses where Paul instructed us to worship in psalms, hymns and spiritual songs:

> **And do not be drunk with wine, in which is dissipation; but be filled with the Spirit, speaking to one another in psalms and hymns and spiritual songs, singing and making melody in your heart to the Lord, giving thanks always for all things to God the Father in the name of our Lord Jesus Christ, submitting to one another in the fear of God.**
> **– Ephesians 5:18-21(NKJ)**

> **Let the word of Christ dwell in you richly in all wisdom; teaching and admonishing one another in psalms and hymns and spiritual songs, singing with grace in your hearts to the Lord.**
> **- Colossians 3:16 (NKJ)**

How To Worship

It may seem selfish to discuss the results of worship in terms of the spiritual benefits to you, but that's not the case. If the use of oxygen becomes necessary during a flight, airplane travelers are instructed to put on their own breath mask first, and then put masks on their children. The reason is if they put the children's on first they may pass out, and then no one will get the air they need.

This principle also applies to your Christian life. You need to make sure you're always built up and strengthened in the Lord, or you won't be able to help the people around you when they need you. Worship is important because it impacts your entire Christian life.

Edification of Self

SPEAKING TO YOURSELVES in psalms and hymns and spiritual songs, singing and making melody in your heart to the Lord; - Ephesians 5:19 (NKJ)

You're not just talking to God when you're singing psalms, hymns and spiritual songs. You're also talking to yourself. When you are worshiping the Lord, obviously you're speaking to Him, but God isn't in Heaven on some kind of ego trip. He's not insecure. He doesn't have low self-esteem. Really, He doesn't even need our praise. So why are we commanded to do it? The answer is that God wants us to praise Him for what it will do for us.

Whether you are singing in tongues or singing in your understanding, you are edifying yourself. To "edify"

Why Should We Do This?

means to build up. Paul taught that *"the one who speaks in a tongue builds up himself..."* (I Corinthians 14:4), and Jude said that *"... you beloved, building yourselves up in your most holy faith and praying in the Holy Spirit"* (Jude 20).

Edification of Others

> **Let the word of Christ dwell in you richly in all wisdom; TEACHING AND ADMONISHING ONE ANOTHER in psalms and hymns and spiritual songs, singing with grace in your hearts to the Lord. - Colossians 3:16 (NKJ)**

When you worship the Lord, you're talking to Him, but you're also talking to the people around you. We generally have a very narrow view of witnessing. We think of witnessing as sharing Jesus with a friend one-on-one, or passing out Gospel tracts. You may not realize it, but your worship is also a witness. When the people around you see you worshiping God, they will be convicted in their own hearts.

This doesn't apply only to sinners, however. When you worship the Lord in spirit and in truth, very often your fellow believers will draw encouragement from that. When the people around you see you worshiping, they will be built up just as you are being built up.

Edification of God

> **Let the word of Christ dwell in you richly in all wisdom; teaching and admonishing one another in psalms and hymns and spiritual**

songs, SINGING with grace in your hearts TO THE LORD. - Colossians 3:16 (NKJ)

Of course, as we examine the benefits of praise and worship – and these are scriptural as we have seen – it's important to remember that worship isn't about us. It's all about Him. The fact that we are able to derive the blessings of worship to ourselves doesn't mean we should ever let the purpose of worship be ,"What's in it for me?"

Our worship is unto Him, by Him, because of Him and for Him. It's okay to divide up the benefits of worship for the individual and for the local church for the purpose of study, but as we do so we must always remember that worship isn't something we do primarily for ourselves, but *"... to the Lord."*

Sustaining Fellowship With God

Speaking to one another in psalms and hymns and spiritual songs, singing and making melody in your heart to the Lord, giving thanks ALWAYS FOR ALL THINGS TO GOD THE FATHER in the name of our Lord Jesus Christ. - Ephesians 5:19-20

You can go all day long worshiping the Lord. This is called practicing the presence of God, which means you train yourself to remember that He's always with you, from the moment you awaken in the morning until you drift off to sleep that evening. When you remember His presence with you during the day, it's natural to want to talk to Him, just as you would want to do with any close friend with whom you were spending the day.

Why Should We Do This?

But in this case it's a Friend who sticks closer than a brother (Proverbs 18:24), who can literally go everywhere with you. Many have asked, "How can we thank God 'always' as the Bible commands?" By learning to practice His presence, you can spend the day worshiping God in your heart.

Ephesians 5:19 can also be read in the sense that you are singing to yourself, or in other words not singing out loud, but quietly in your heart. Sometimes, if you're at work for example, it wouldn't be appropriate to sing praises out loud. Yet you can still have a song in your heart, where you go throughout the day fellowshipping with Him as your praise builds you up spiritually.

Summary

God has established praise and worship so that we may enjoy the benefits of worshiping Him, and these many benefits should help motivate us to worship Him more. While we must remember that the purpose of worshiping Him isn't just to obtain the benefits, we must also understand that the benefits have a purpose.

Aside from just being a blessing to you personally, the benefits help you to gauge where you are spiritually when you worship Him. How can you know that you're truly worshiping God in spirit and in truth? How can you be certain that you've engaged in authentic worship? The presence or absence of the benefits of worship can help guide you:

Often it's not what happens during worship, but

How To Worship

what occurs after worship which confirms whether or not you've been engaged in authentic worship. How is your character and attitude? After spending time in His presence, are you motivated to love Him more? David sang, *"I have stored up your word in my heart, that I might not sin against you."* (Psalms 119:11).

What about others? After a session of worshiping the Lord, are you provoked to walk in love more, and to forgive those who may have slighted you? What about those outside the church? Do they sense something different about you that they can't quite put their finger on, but that you know is the presence of God manifested in your life in a stronger way because He has inhabited your praises?

This book was intentionally written to instruct you *How to Worship,* not to catalog the many benefits of worship. Yet, you should be able to see now that even the benefits of worship, by virtue of their presence or absence in your life, can help you become more mature in how you worship. These benefits not only motivate us to worship, but also assist us immeasurably when it comes to calibrating and fine tuning our own worship technique.

Why Should We Do This?

Chapter 7 Discussion Questions

1. Group discussion: Share a divine encounter experienced at your church during corporate worship.

2. Does understanding the specific benefits of praise and worship motivate you to do it more? How does it affect your expectations for the next worship service you will attend?

3. What are some reasons you might be reluctant (or have been in the past) to "practice" praise?

4. How do the individual benefits of praise and worship help us gauge where we are in our spiritual growth? Are the benefits of authentic worship seen only during worship time, or do they show up afterward as well?

5. What are some of the ways worshiping with psalms, hymns and spiritual songs can help us to edify ourselves?

6. David wrote in Psalm 119:11: *"Your word have I hidden in my heart that I might not sin against you."* How does praise move us from a place of information in our minds, to Illumination within our spirit? How does that lead us to more authentic worship?

Chapter 8

Getting Started
Examples of Worship

Let no one despise you for your youth, but set the believers an example in speech, in conduct, in love, in faith, in purity. – I Timothy 4:12

Assuming you've read the previous seven chapters in order as recommended, at this point the place of praise and worship in your life should be very clear to you. "Okay, you've convinced me," you say. "Worship is important and it needs to be part of my spiritual life. But I feel like I'm so unskilled at it. Where do I begin?"

If this is your heart's cry, I have good news. The Bible is literally FULL of examples you can easily emulate until you're comfortable worshiping creatively on your own.

Precepts

The Bible talks about two different ways to learn: by precept and example. Learning by precept involves exposing yourself to anointed teaching that helps you to assemble new knowledge and revelation brick by brick, starting with the foundation and working up. This is a scriptural method of instruction. The prophet Isaiah taught this way.

> **For it is precept upon precept,**
> **precept upon precept,**
> **line upon line, line upon line,**
> **here a little, there a little. - Isaiah 28:10**

Different people learn in different ways. Some people can be given a set of instructions to read and they'll be good to go. Others aren't able to "get it" by just reading about it, but if they can observe someone else doing it then they can figure it out from there. Better still, if one can watch an expert perform with precision and excellence, his own performance will improve dramatically.

Examples

The first seven chapters of *How To Worship* have been by precept. Now it's time for some examples. As we look to the Word of God for examples of worship, keep in mind that these were frail, fallible, imperfect people just like you. If they were able to enter into the presence of God with their praise, there's no reason why you can't do it too.

Maybe you've stood beside someone in church at some point and overheard them praising God, and you thought to yourself, "Wow, he's really good at that," or "I wish I was able to praise God that smoothly." Now it's time for you to become that person whom others look to for guidance and as an example of worship.

Much of the rest of this chapter will be scripture

references, with only limited commentary. The goal is to give you ideas that you can use which will help you develop into a more skillful worshiper.

The Psalms

The Book of Psalms is an excellent place to find some great examples of praise. It's easy to imagine yourself standing in church, with your hands raised in worship, saying these words out loud:

O Lord, our Lord,
**   how majestic is your name in all the earth!**
You have set your glory above the heavens.
**   - Psalm 8:1**

Lord, you have been our dwelling place
**   in all generations.**
Before the mountains were brought forth, or
**   ever you had formed the earth and the world,**
**   from everlasting to everlasting you are God.**
**   - Psalm 90:2**

Yet you are holy, enthroned on the praises of Israel. - Psalm 22:3

You have turned for me my mourning into dancing; you have loosed my sackcloth and clothed me with gladness, - Psalm 30:11

I will bless the Lord at all times; his praise shall continually be in my mouth. - Psalm 34:1

How To Worship

> I will sing of steadfast love and justice; to you, O Lord, I will make music. - Psalm 101:1

> I will give to the Lord the thanks due to his righteousness, and I will sing praise to the name of the Lord, the Most High. - Psalm 7:17

> Praise the Lord! Praise the Lord from the heavens; praise him in the heights! Praise him, all his angels; praise him, all his hosts! Praise him, sun and moon, praise him, all you shining stars! Praise him, you highest heavens, and you waters above the heavens! Let them praise the name of the Lord! For he commanded and they were created. - Psalm 148:1-5

> I will extol you, O Lord, for you have drawn me up and have not let my foes rejoice over me.
>   - Psalm 30:1

The Writings of the Prophets

Another excellent source of praise examples is in the writings of the Prophets. Under the Old Covenant, these men walked closer to the Lord than anyone else.

> I will give thanks to you, O Lord,
>   for though you were angry with me,
> your anger turned away,
>   that you might comfort me. - Isaiah 12:1

> O Lord, you are my God;
>   I will exalt you; I will praise your name,

Getting Started

for you have done wonderful things,
  plans formed of old, faithful and sure.
    - Isaiah 25:1

Sing to the Lord a new song,
  his praise from the end of the earth,
you who go down to the sea, and all that fills it,
  the coastlands and their inhabitants.
    - Isaiah 42:10

Heal me, O Lord, and I shall be healed;
  save me, and I shall be saved,
  for you are my praise. - Jeremiah 17:14

Sing to the Lord; praise the Lord!
For he has delivered the life of the needy
  from the hand of evildoers. - Jeremiah 20:13

Blessed be the name of God forever and ever,
  to whom belong wisdom and might.
He changes times and seasons;
  he removes kings and sets up kings;
he gives wisdom to the wise and
  knowledge to those who have understanding;
he reveals deep and hidden things;
  he knows what is in the darkness,
  and the light dwells with him.
To you, O God of my fathers,
  I give thanks and praise,
for you have given me wisdom and might, and
  have now made known to me what we asked of
you, for you have made known to us the king's
matter. - Daniel 2:20-23

The Canticles

Luke's Gospel contains three songs, called canticles: The *Magnificat* (The Song of Mary in Luke 1:46-55), *The Benedictus* (the Song of Zechariah in Luke 1:68-79), and *Nunc Dimittis* (The Song of Simeon in Luke 2:29-32). The traditional names ascribed to them are based on their open lines in the Latin text.

All three canticles can be heard on the Internet if you're interested, but for our purposes we just want to see if we can learn from their example in our own worship. Let's take a look at the *Magnificat,* the song of a very young girl which followed her conversation with the angel Gabriel:

> **My soul magnifies the Lord,**
> **And my spirit has rejoiced in God my Savior.**
> **For He who is mighty has done great things**
>   **for me,**
> **And holy is His name.**
> **And His mercy is on those who fear Him**
> **From generation to generation.**
> **He has shown strength with His arm;**
> **He has scattered the proud in the imagination**
>   **of their hearts.**
> **He has put down the mighty from their**
>   **thrones,**
> **And exalted the lowly.**
> **He has filled the hungry with good things,**
> **And the rich He has sent away empty.**
> **He has helped His servant Israel,**
> **In remembrance of His mercy,**
> **As He spoke to our fathers,**

To Abraham and to his seed forever.
   - Luke 1:46-47, 49-55

In taking this passage as an example of worship there are a few things that should be noted. First off, this praise was originally specific to Mary and her situation, and while we can emulate Mary as an outstanding example of praise, verse 48 applies to only Mary herself, so it was left out of the example above. Sometimes you will need to do this so you can fashion the praise for your own use.

Another thing to be aware of is there are many passages like this one where you can substitute the word "You" for "He," enabling you to address the Lord in worship directly. This makes the praise less abstract and more personal to you. For example, you could change verse 49 like so:

*"For **You** who are mighty has done great things for me, and holy is **Your** name."*

Praises in Heaven

Heaven is a real place, and it is another great source of ideas for how to get started with your own praise and worship. There's no place on Earth where they praise God like they do in the Holy City, and because of that we can learn to praise God not just from our fellow believers who have gone on ahead of us, but from other heavenly beings as well:

Holy, holy, holy is the Lord of hosts;
The whole earth is full of His glory!
   - Isaiah 6:3

How To Worship

Many Christians don't read the Book of Revelation because it scares them, but in that book are a great many wonderful examples of worship that we can use as a pattern for our own praise:

Holy, holy, holy, Lord God Almighty, Who was and is and is to come! - Revelation 4:8

Thou art worthy, O Lord, to receive glory and honor and power: for thou hast created all things, and for thy pleasure they are and were created. - Revelation 4:11 (KJV)

Worthy is the Lamb who was slain to receive power and wealth and wisdom, and might and honor and glory and blessing! - Revelation 5:12

Blessing and honor and glory and power be to Him who sits on the throne, and to the Lamb, forever and ever! - Revelation 5:13 (NKJ)

Amen! Blessing and glory and wisdom, thanksgiving and honor and power and might be to our God forever and ever. Amen. - Revelation 7:12

**Great and marvelous are Your works, Lord God Almighty! Just and true are Your ways, O King of the saints! Who shall not fear You, O Lord, and glorify Your name? For You alone are holy. For all nations shall come and worship before You. For Your judgments have been manifested.
- Revelation 15:3-4**

Getting Started

There are many more examples of praise in the Word of God, but space does not permit us to look at them all. Until you become comfortable praising God spontaneously on your own, why not take some of these examples of praise and emulate them? You can also take elements of these verses and mix and match them. Here's an example of what your praise might sound like when you worship God this way:

"Lord, you are holy. There is none like you in Heaven or on the Earth. From everlasting to everlasting you are God. You are wise. You are mighty. You are loving, full of grace and mercy. I praise you. I worship you. Thank you for your goodness toward me. All power, all might, all dominion, all authority, be unto you, King of Kings and Lord of Lords. The whole earth is full of your glory. Hallelujah!"

Summary

The Bible is comprised of books written by men who were inspired by the Holy Spirit (II Peter 1:20-21). That means the worship examples found within the pages of God's Word are literally Holy Spirit-inspired praises. What better source of praise and worship training could you find than that?

One of the best ways to learn is by example, and there are no better examples of praise and worship than those which can be found inside the Bible itself. Take advantage of these examples, and use them to "fake it until you make it" - that is, until you are comfortable praising God on your own.

How To Worship

It's not about impressing others, although it's not impossible that you could become such a capable "praiser" that God would use you as an example for your brothers and sisters who are less experienced in worship. That may seem like an outlandish possibility to you, but I assure you that it's absolutely possible.

True spiritual growth, in any area, not just worship, involves passing through four separate phases:

1) Unconscious incompetence – you're not any good, but you don't know how bad you are

2) Conscious incompetence – you're still not any good, but now you're aware that you aren't good

3) Conscious competence – you are improving, but you have to work hard at it on purpose to be good

4) Unconscious competence – you are continually improving without ever having to think about it

What it's really all about is being able to come before your Heavenly Father with confidence, not worrying whether the worship you're about to give Him will sound foolish or elementary, but knowing that you've applied yourself to become a true worshiper in spirit and in truth, and that you're continually growing in grace as a worshiper all the time. Worship the Lord in His temple, and go forth rejoicing!

Now may the God of peace himself sanctify you completely, and may your whole spirit and soul and body be kept blameless at the coming of our Lord Jesus Christ. - I Thessalonians 5:23

Chapter 8 Discussion Questions

1. What advice would you give to a new Christian who's exposed to charismatic praise and worship for the first time? What would you say to someone who didn't want to be thought of as "weird?"

2. What are some of your favorite verses of Scripture that you like to incorporate into your praise?

3. How else might you personalize Bible verses? In what situations do you think that might be helpful to you?

4. How is praise and worship similar to giving a testimony? How is it different? Who is the audience and what is the intended effect of each one?

5. When having a conversation, are you always in control? Should you then always be in control during praise and worship? What are the benefits of setting aside your personal agenda when you enter into praise and worship?

6. Who in your life is a model or mentor for your Christian walk? How do those persons express themselves in praise and worship? Do you think they reached that point randomly, or was it a result of their dedication? In what ways can emulating them help increase your spiritual growth?

Conclusion

In *How To Worship* the meaning behind worshiping God in spirit and in truth has been revealed as worshiping God authentically with a pure heart, and worshiping Him according to the methods given within the Word of God.

Thanksgiving, praise and worship have been defined as three distinct and progressive phases of worship, and the differences and similarities between them have been examined.

The true New Testament temple has been identified, recognizing that it's not a building made of natural materials, but a spiritual building made up of all believers corporately, and that your spirit, soul and body make up your temple of the Holy Spirit individually.

Thanksgiving in the Outer Court of the body was explored, with scriptural examples given for what you should do with your body when you worship.

Praise in the Inner Court of the soul was examined, and from the seven Hebrew words for praise we learned how to focus our own soul and protect ourselves from distractions when we worship.

The next thing taught was how to experience

How To Worship

worship in the Holy of Holies of your spirit, through the singing of psalms, hymns and spiritual songs.

After that, we identified some of the benefits of praise and worship, and we examined how the presence of those blessings helps us gauge how we're progressing in authentic worship.

Finally, practical examples of worship from the Bible were reviewed, which you can follow as you begin your own experience as a worshiper in spirit and in truth.

I trust you've enjoyed reading *How To Worship* as much as I've enjoyed writing it. Would you believe that after reading this book, it wouldn't be an exaggeration at all to say that you now know more about worship than most of the Christians in the world today?

But now that you have learned how to worship, you can teach others through your example. I hope you won't let the things you've learned become just a bunch of concepts and theory, but rather that you will begin to put this new revelation into practice in your own life so that your worship might bring you ever closer to Almighty God, the Creator of Heaven and Earth.

Conclusion

Closing Prayer

Heavenly Father, I thank You for the grace you've given me to write this book. I pray that I've been able to bring it forth as You wanted it brought forth, and I ask that any mistakes or errors on my part would be overshadowed by the teaching ministry of the Holy Spirit for the readers.

For those who have read *How To Worship,* I pray that the revelations they've gained won't be just information and data in their heads, but impartations of truth within their hearts and spirits. I pray You will encourage them as they begin to spread their wings in worship, and draw near to them as they draw near to You.

In the mighty Name of the Lord Jesus Christ I pray.

Amen.

Scripture Index

Reference	Page
Genesis 2:7	37, 78
Exodus 15:11	25
Exodus 15:1-21	79
Exodus 25	33
Exodus 25:8	35
Exodus 37:6-9	35
I Samuel 10:5	88
I Samuel 16:16	72
I Samuel 16:23	72
II Samuel 22	79
II Samuel 6:14	52
I Chronicles 25:1	88
II Chronicles 20:19-23	63
Job 38:7	71
Psalm 4:1	80
Psalm 5:7	53
Psalm 7:17	23, 110
Psalm 8:1	109
Psalm 8:2	95
Psalm 22:3	73, 95, 109
Psalm 23	81
Psalm 30:1	110
Psalm 30:11	109
Psalm 30:11, 12	51
Psalm 34:1	109
Psalm 35:18	22
Psalm 44:1, 2	5
Psalm 46:10	70
Psalm 47:1	48
Psalm 50:14	55
Psalm 50:23	63
Psalm 63:1-3	67
Psalm 63:5	62
Psalm 65:4	38
Psalm 72:14, 15	69
Psalm 72:20	69
Psalm 79:13	27
Psalm 89:6-7	15
Psalm 86:9, 10	27
Psalm 90:2	109
Psalm 95:6	69
Psalm 100:4	21, 39, 64
Psalm 101:1	110
Psalm 102:18-22	9
Psalm 103:1-5	60
Psalm 106:47	26
Psalm 113:1-3	65
Psalm 114	66
Psalm 117:1	67
Psalms 119:11	104
Psalm 132:7	43
Psalm 133	98
Psalm 135:2	47
Psalm 138:2	17, 33
Psalm 148:1-5	110
Psalm 149:1	70
Psalm 149:3	72
Psalm 149:1-4	46
Proverbs 14:12	16
Proverbs 18:24	103
Isaiah 6:3	113
Isaiah 12:1	110

Isaiah 12:4	22	I Corinthians 6:19-20	37
Isaiah 25:1	110	I Corinthians 12:28	45
Isaiah 28:10	108	I Corinthians 14:4	101
Isaiah 29:13	13	I Corinthians 14:15	35, 87
Isaiah 42:10	111	II Corinthians 3:17	96
Isaiah 45:15	96	II Corinthians 5:8	78
Jeremiah 17:14	111	II Corinthians 5:17	78
Jeremiah 20:13	111	Ephesians 5:2	35
Daniel 2:20-23	111	Ephesians 5:17-21	77
Zephaniah 3:17	71	Ephesians 5:18	81
Matthew 5:48	74	Ephesians 5:18-21	99
Matthew 7:13, 14	17	Ephesians 5:19	100, 103
Matthew 21:16	95	Ephesians 5:19, 20	102
Matthew 27:50, 51	35, 40	Ephesians 5:21	97
Matthew 26:30	85	Ephesians 5:26	34, 56
Mark 4:35-41	69	Philippians 2:6-1	85
Mark 7:13	6	Colossians 1:15-20	85
Luke 1:46-47	112	Colossians 2:6, 7	94
Luke 1:49-55	112	Colossians 3:16	93, 98, 99
Luke 1:68-79	85		101, 102
Luke 21:19	61, 92	I Thessalonians 5:19	96
John 4:23, 24	11, 12, 18, 78	I Thessalonians 5:23	38, 116
John 6:35	35	I Timothy 2:8	49, 54
John 14:26	7	I Timothy 3:16	85
John 17:1	53	I Timothy 4:12	107
John 17:17	15	Hebrews 2:12	82
Acts 4:24	64	Hebrews 9:3, 4	35
Acts 10:38	96, 98	Hebrews 9:12	40
Acts 16:25	85	Hebrews 9:12-14	34
Acts 17:23	17	Hebrews 12:28, 29	14
Romans 1:21	14	Hebrews 13:15	44, 63
I Corinthians 3:16, 17	36	James 1:17	50
I Corinthians 6:19-20	37	James 1:22	89

Scripture Index

James 3:16	97
I Peter 2:5	36
II Peter 1:3	21
II Peter 1:20, 21	115
I John 4:8	97
Jude 20	101
Revelation 4:8	114
Revelation 4:11	114
Revelation 5:8	35
Revelation 5:11, 12	28
Revelation 5:12	114
Revelation 5:13	114
Revelation 7:12	114
Revelation 15:3, 4	114
Revelation 19:6, 7	59

How Can I Be Saved?

Are you ready to accept the gift of eternal life that Jesus is offering you right now? If you sincerely desire to receive Jesus into your heart as your Lord and Savior, then here's a suggested prayer you can pray. You don't have to use these exact words. What's most important is that you're talking to God from your heart:

> *"Lord Jesus, I know that I am a sinner and I do not deserve eternal life. But, I believe You died and rose from the grave to make me a new creation and to prepare me to dwell in your presence forever. Jesus, come into my life, take control of my life, forgive my sins and save me. I am now placing my trust in You alone for my salvation and I accept your free gift of eternal life."*

Congratulations! You've just been adopted into the family of God. Since the theme of this book is largely focused on the unseen spirit realm, you should be aware of what the angels are doing right now, according to Jesus:

> **Just so, I tell you, there is joy before the angels of God over one sinner who repents. – Luke 15:10**

If you've prayed this prayer for the first time, please contact me at *praisereport@michaeldorseyonline.org* so we can celebrate with you!

About the Author

Saved at the age of 10 and Spirit-filled at age 16, Rev. Michael Dorsey has been a Christian for more than 30 years, and a teacher of the Word of God for over 20 of those years. He has ministered to new believers one-on-one, taught various Bible courses, and has been a speaker at ministers conferences.

Michael is the author of several books, including the multi-volume *How To Live* series. He has been called of God to provide quality outreach materials for true seekers, to build up and strengthen new believers, and to train up mature Christians for more effective service.

His passion is discipling new believers, teaching them the Word of God so they can be transformed from victims into victorious Christians, and then equipping those believers to begin discipling others to the glory of God.

Michael and his wife Katherine, along with their children Robbie and Kirsten, are active partners with Riverside Church in the Baltimore area, where they work in the ministry and assist their Pastor to bless God's people.

THANK YOU!

I hope you've enjoyed this book, *How To Worship - Entering Into and Enjoying the Presence of God*, the ninth volume in the *How To Live* series. Now you're ready to take your praise life to the next level of glory in Christ Jesus!

As a personal thank you for reading *How To Worship*, I'd like to invite you to visit the this website:

www.howtoworshipbook.com/thankyou

where you will find additional free resources available for you to download that will further assist you in your daily worship. Once again, thank you so much for your support and your prayers!

Michael Dorsey

How To Worship

Entering Into and Enjoying the Presence of God

is a publication of

For further information on
the How To Live series,
along with details of other
publications and upcoming projects
designed to equip Christians
to live victoriously,
please visit us at:

www.malakimpress.com

www.ingramcontent.com/pod-product-compliance
Lightning Source LLC
Chambersburg PA
CBHW071702040426
42446CB00011B/1872